By Freedom's Holy Light

BY FREEDOM'S HOLY LIGHT

A Selection of Patriotic Messages by

Gordon Palmer, D.D.; Litt. D.

With a Foreword by

JOHN W. BRADBURY, D.D.

THE DEVIN-ADAIR COMPANY

New York • 1964

Foreword

THROUGHOUT these post-war years there has been evidence of a growing need for voices that interpret the ideals of the Republic to our American people. Dr. Palmer's has become such a voice.

The chapters of this book consist of messages delivered by Dr. Gordon Palmer over a wide network of radio stations. A reading of these messages will evoke admiration for their consistency and their high ethical standard. One can easily see why they have received special recognition by patriotic organizations.

The background of Dr. Palmer eminently qualifies him for the distinguished role he now fills. His ministry has been and is, a wide one, including a chaplaincy to the 13th U. S. Infantry, pastorates of several large churches, service as chaplain to the California American Legion, presidency of Eastern Baptist Theological Seminary in Philadelphia and lecturer at institutions of learning, churches, conferences and other places of service.

In an era of tension in the country, because of the threat of Communism from without and within, Dr. Palmer instituted a radio program entitled Christian Patriotism Ministry. Year after year he has kept this service for God and country going forward with a high standard of instruction and inspiration. Ten awards from Freedom Foundation with

George Washington medals and two awards from the All-American Conference to Combat Communism, are among the many honors accorded him.

Our nation's foundation is Christian and there can be no doubt of our country's faith in God. It is part of the warp and woof of our national pattern. The fact that over 117,-000,000 of our American people are identified with some church indicates that the great majority of our citizens desire that our religious foundations shall sustain the ideals of Godliness and liberty in the land.

Communism with its atheism has no rightful place among the American people. The climactic evil of undiluted Marxism has blossomed and borne evil fruit in Communist tyranny. It has enslaved hundreds of millions and deluded many more. Some estimate that fully one-third of the inhabitants of the world are in its grip. Its discipline is a rifle bullet, its law is without justice, its politics knows no democracy, its fictitious economics is based on conscription, its domestic application is with strict partiality, its mentality is limited by a relentless and magnified negative.

Communism is anti-religious because it dreads what faith in God may lead people to do; it attempts to care for the body while crushing the soul, and it leads its victims down to the bottomless pit which they enter without God and without hope.

The most effective defense a free people may have against Communism's delusions is a positive Christian faith. Our Founding Fathers were grounded in this faith. Our Declaration of Independence is a substantial exhibition of its verities. Our American Constitution is a corporate expression of principles of national and social well-being which stem from the same faith. Our multitude of institutions, our vast cluster of brotherhoods, our local, county, state and national freedoms; our moral and spiritual purpose to repress exploiters, to promote justice, to raise the standard of living and to spread happiness in a general well-being—all indicate the flow of blessings which come from God through the deeds of His good men. Throughout the world America is known for this. We are His witnesses.

At the same time there has been a vast flow of Communist ideas constantly washing over our borders. These seek our liberty in order to destroy us. They deny our faith and encourage the undermining forces which would restrict our freedom. The special end of this drive is the striking down of the Free Enterprise System, which is the economic expression of our national freedom and prosperity.

To constructively serve the American people in defense of the faith and its free expression in active living, Dr. Palmer can now be heard over twenty-nine radio stations every Sunday. This selection from his messages which have been sent over the airwaves to hundreds of thousands, if not millions of people is an important contribution. Those who have heard and longed to possess copies of them may now have their wish realized in this book. Dr. Palmer's words are good food for the minds of patriotic Americans. They will brighten every life and every home they enter.

JOHN W. BRADBURY

New York City

Contents

Preface

THIS BOOK HAS GROWN out of the messages given over the radio in certain largely populated areas of our country. They are intended to be positive, with the aim of exalting the good elements in the life of Americans and of America.

Too many people, at home and abroad, have tried to downgrade our country and to make the "Ugly American" the picture of all Americans. Negations do not build. Therefore, I have dealt with positives. No other country has been so profligate in giving money, men and assistance to all nations, large and small—even to her professed enemies—and without any demand for possessions in return. America has been the "good Samaritan of nations" and has become the "head servant in the household of the world," just as W. E. Gladstone, the "Grand Old Man" of England, prophesied.

This book goes out with thanksgiving to God for what America has done for and meant to the author, who is a naturalized citizen and proud of it. We pray that these messages will strengthen the faith of patriots and correct the unhappy criticisms of the pessimists.

We express our thanks to Dr. John W. Bradbury of *The Watchman-Examiner* for reading the script, correcting it and arranging for its publication, to Mr. D. A. Garrity of The Devin-Adair Company for review and oversight of its production, to Mr. William George, manager of Radio

KGER, Long Beach, California, for the encouragement by his staff in helping to make the broadcasts possible, to our daughter, Janet, who typed the manuscript and finally for the large number of those who have requested that these messages be published.

GORDON PALMER

Los Angeles, California

By Freedom's Holy Light

I

Has America
Outgrown the Bible?

> All scripture is given by inspiration of God, and is
> profitable for doctrine, for reproof, for correction,
> for instruction in righteousness: That the man of
> God may be perfect, thoroughly furnished unto
> all good works.
>
> —*2 Timothy, 3:16–17*

BECAUSE OF PUBLIC CONCERN over the decision
of the Supreme Court, which had the effect of declaring
Bible reading in the public schools for devotion and spiritual and character building purposes to be unconstitutional,
the question has been raised, "Has America outgrown the
Bible?" We need to consider the answer to that.

The Bible is a miraculous book. It outlives all others. It
is supreme in its message, incomparable in its wisdom, and
is the most audacious statement of truth ever written. It
has built up nations and corrected empires. It has made and
unmade civilizations. It has wrecked philosophies and
overthrown superstitions. A transforming light breaks

forth from its pages. Heathenism cannot withstand its re-creative force, nor ignorance its power of illumination.

The rock foundation upon which the United States is built is the Bible. Although some men, by word or by attitude, indicate that America has outgrown the Bible, nevertheless, we cannot escape our debt to its influence in our remarkable history. The Bible is the Constitution of Christian civilization. From the courageous Pilgrim Fathers, to our presidents, statesmen, scholars, literary men, military geniuses, educators, and captains of industry, men have been captivated with the mighty spiritual power, the stirring emotional appeal, and the strong intellectual challenge of the Bible.

Today, we seem to read everything but the Bible, yet it is still the world's best-seller. California has closed the door of the school against it as a spiritual and character building agency, yet officials keep on wondering how to solve the social and moral problems of youth. Do we think we have become intellectually superior to the Bible? Do we consider ourselves morally, educationally, and spiritually self-sufficient? What if nearly everybody said, "We have outgrown the Bible?" That would still not be evidence that it was true.

A DYNAMIC POWER

Because the world has never been courageous enough to live out the standards, ideals, and principles contained in the Bible, that is no argument against the dynamics of these teachings. Men everywhere have been slow to grasp or to accept its truths. The Bible throws out the most astounding and startling challenges ever hurled at humanity. Wherever the Bible goes there is always a revival of faith or a revolution. An open Bible means enlightened souls. There is dynamite in the Bible. It blasts away the darkened prison walls of ignorance and slavery, and lets in the light of liberty and justice.

An open Bible proclaims liberty and demands justice. The world today needs more justice in every human relationship. We have not outgrown the Bible in this respect, because the Bible is the manual of justice. It teaches what justice is and how it should be given. The Bible is the chart for our day. It is the lamp for our times of perplexity. It is the light to our path out of the gloom of national and international misunderstanding.

The Bible is the precursor of progress. Those nations have forged ahead that have attempted to fuse its moral, social and religious truths and ideals into personal and national life. They who build on the Bible construct on rock foundations. Its truths, like Gibraltar, are impregnable, unshakable. They are eternal.

The Bible is the most daring book for a daring age. It furnishes great adventure for adventurous youth. It inspires. It encourages men to attempt impossibilities and furnishes power to accomplish them.

Science has advanced but it has not outgrown the Bible. There are no grounds of disagreement between the ascertained facts of science and the correct understanding of statements of the Bible. There is a tremendous difference between the proven facts of science and undemonstrated guesses. So-called facts of science change as often as the moon. Theories which, yesterday, scientists declared were final, will tomorrow be cast into the morgue of discarded scientific suppositions. Withhold hasty condemnation until all the facts are in. When that time comes it will be found that true science accords with the truths of revealed religion. *Both are from God and God cannot contradict Himself.* The skeptic, of all men, is the most inconsistent and most unreasonable. He accepts daily as facts, things which in the realm of religion he denies. In religion, he demands demonstration every step of the way, but in everyday dealings, he acts on faith. Science demands tests. The Bible stands the test. Try it.

THE BIBLE ENDURES THE CHANGES OF TIME

Material things do not make national greatness. The palaces of Greece have gone, but the poetic ideals of Homer remain. The Caesars have passed on and the Coliseum is in ruins, but Rome's ideals of law and literature live. It is not the material things that endure. Moral and spiritual ideals abide. Our ideals and true national greatness are due to the Bible. Until higher ideals than those found in the New Testament are created, America can never outgrow the Bible.

Has America outgrown the Golden Rule? Can a higher ethic of honesty and fair dealing with men be found than that in the Sermon on the Mount? Is there a more sane and sensible manner of overcoming race prejudice than that exemplified by Jesus Christ on the basis of Christian brotherhood? Where is a higher ideal for man or nation than, "The son of man came not to be ministered unto, but to minister and give his life a ransom for many?" Where is there found a higher value placed upon man than that given by Jesus Christ; not "a worm of the dust," but a potential son of God? Where has woman received more liberty and more gracious consideration than where the Bible is loved, honored and exalted? And where have little children a higher consideration in the thought and legislation of nations than where the name of Jesus is loved and worshipped? Has America outgrown these ideals?

While the Grand Old Book is the center of attack by unbelievers, nevertheless there is plenty of evidence that the Bible has not been destroyed.

The Bible is still the most popular book in the world. Almost every newspaper with a worthy reputation gives a prominent place daily to some great passage of Scripture. Editorials are more frequently written upon the Bible than ever before in history. Now, never a day passes but that the Bible is read over the radio morning, noon, and night. The prophecy of the Bible has been fulfilled so that "the knowledge of the Lord covers the earth as the waters cover the sea." No book has ever been so widely translated. The whole Bible has been translated into 200 languages, the New Testament into 250 languages, the Gospels, verses, and parts of the Bible into over 1,100 tongues and dialects.

Men may cry, "Scrap the Bible." Scrap the Bible, and we might as well throw American civilization on the junkpile. Neglect the Bible, and we court the hand of the infidel. Ridicule the Bible, and we flirt with anarchy and atheistic Communism in a most deadly form. Unbelief does not construct. Atheism never builds. Infidelity weakens the foundations. A sneer at the Bible is a strike at Christianity.

We run a serious risk when we send to public office any man who makes light of the Bible, or who ignores the teachings of Jesus Christ.

The Rajah of Travancore in India once gave this testimony: "Where do the English get their knowledge, intelligence, cleverness, and power? It is from the Bible, which gives it to them. Now they have translated it into our own language, bring it to us and say, *'take it, read it, examine it, and see if it is not good!'* Of one thing I am convinced. Do what we will, oppose it as we may, it is the Christian Bible that will sooner or later work out the regeneration of our land."

NEEDED MORE THAN EVER

In the light of the recent decisions of the Supreme Court, America needs the message of the Bible more than ever. The lone dissenting Justice deserves praise for his courage to declare himself in favor of Bible reading for spiritual and moral character building in the public schools, as had been for 170 years. This made Bible reading a living, vital tradition of the American way of life. The Bible guides the total life of our country, because it points the way to life, liberty, and the pursuit of happiness. Note the unusual document which was given to me when visiting Westminster Abbey in London. This document was discovered in the Abbey generations ago. Its truth lives, and America and Americans need to follow its challenge.

A nation would be truly blessed if it were governed by no other laws than this blessed Book. It is so complete a system that nothing needs be added to it or taken from it. It affords a copy for a king and a rule for a subject. It gives instruction and counsel to the Senate, authority and direction to the magistrate. It cautions the witness, requires impartial verdict from the jury, and it furnishes the judge with a sentence. It entails honor to the parent, enjoins obedience to children. It prescribes and limits the sway of a sovereign, the rule of the ruler, and the authority of the master. It commands the subjects to honor and the servants to obey. It promises the blessing and protection of its author to all who walk by its rules. It defends the rights of all. It reveals vengeance to every defrauder, over-reacher, and oppressor.

It is the first Book and the best Book in the world. It contains the choicest matter, gives the best instruction, and affords the greatest pleasure and satisfaction that can be revealed. It contains the best laws, the profoundest mysteries that ever were published. It brings the best of tidings, and affords the best of comfort to the inquiring and disconsolate. In short, it is a book of laws to show right from wrong, a book of wisdom that condemns all folly and makes the foolish wise. It is a book that detects all lies and confronts all errors, a book of life that shows the way from everlasting death to everlasting life.

Americans can never outgrow such a book of wisdom, counsel and encouragement. We are confident that its message will be forever living and ever new. "My word shall not return unto me void but it can accomplish that which I please and it shall prosper in the thing whereunto I have sent it" (*Isaiah 55:11*).

America will never fail under the most severe of testings if we make its message and its truth our own and obey its commands, and do the will of God as required therein.

America has not outgrown the Bible. However, we warn our beloved country: "Scrap the Bible, and in its place we shall build a scaffold upon which to hang American civilization." God forbid!

2

Righteousness and Freedom

> The integrity of the upright shall guide them: but the perverseness of transgressors shall destroy them.
>
> —*Proverbs 11 : 3*

> Wear integrity as your coat of mail.
>
> —*Ephesians 6 : 14*
> *(Moffatt)*

IT WAS SOLOMON who wrote: "The integrity of the upright shall guide them: but the perverseness of transgressors shall destroy them." In the New Testament Paul wrote: "Wear integrity as your coat of mail." These declarations are eternally true. They represent the heart of Jesus' practical gospel. Christ demonstrated God's full Word in his own speech, life and deeds. Jesus was and is the perfect example of absolute integrity.

Paul the Apostle was speaking of Christ's perfect integrity when he exhorted the Ephesians to "wear integrity as your coat of mail." He must have been well aware of the high importance of this quality in the lives of prophets and kings as well as of ordinary citizens.

Integrity is the keystone in the arch of triumph of all American freedoms and the Christian free-enterprise way of life. Great concern is being expressed in magazine and newspaper editorials and by radio commentators over what they call "moral decadence" or "a breakdown in common morality." This concern is most healthful. When ministers speak of the downgrading of American morality, some people call them "dispensers of gloom." But most newspaper correspondents and editors are keen realists and when they write as they are doing about immorality in every phase of life, we believe their concern is promising for an awakened citizenry.

Too many Americans have been living in a fool's paradise, thinking there is nothing wrong in our governmental, political, social and educational life. If we are to awaken Americans to their obligations and responsibilities, there is a need for someone to be "the watchman on the tower" crying, "What of the night?"

In W. Somerset Maugham's book, *Of Human Bondage*, he makes his leading character, Philip Carey, say, "Follow your inclinations with due respect to the policeman around the corner." What he apparently meant was, be shrewd; do not put all your best goods in the window; keep your conscience a little asleep; lie a little, here and there, if you can get away with it; cheat, now and then, so long as no one sees you. But this cannot keep going on without wrecking our character; and of the character of a nation. God says: "Integrity of the upright shall guide them: but the perverseness of transgressors shall destroy them."

THE BASIC VIRTUE

Integrity is the basic virtue in Christian American leadership that can and will, under God, keep America in the foremost leadership for world goodwill, understanding and peace.

America has been building an "Arc de Triomphe" on a "Champs-Elysées" of world civilization, and the keystone in that arch has been and must ever be "integrity," spelled out in character and ideals in the lives of its citizens. Integrity is also the keystone in the arch of national and international brotherliness. There seems no quality of righteousness or of integrity in the thinking or philosophy of world atheism. *Senate Document No. 125 (84th Congress, May 21, 1956)* is a record of systematic diplomatic treachery. There is a list of more than 1,000 treaties of peace, amity, and commerce which, without conscience, have been violated and repudiated by Communist Russia since 1917. Well might Mr. Eisenhower have said to Bulganin, as he did on August 4, 1956: "I must confess that I am perplexed as to how we can work together constructively if agreements which are negotiated at the highest level, after the most thorough exploration, do not seem to be dependable." (*Department of Publication 6972, April 1960, p. 71*).

There is no basis of brotherly fellowship when one or more of the parties cannot be trusted. Again, integrity must be the keystone in the arch of successful diplomatic relations.

In the area of our country's domestic felicity, integrity is imperative. Something seems to have happened in some of the places of leadership in our beloved America. Our government demands the strictest integrity of its citizens in paying taxes and in obedience to its laws. But consider this quote from *Consumers' Reports*, (*March 1961, p. 120*): "Getting honest ham for your Easter dinner this year is going to be a matter of luck and it will have to be good luck, because the cards are now heavily stacked against the ham buyer. On the 30th of last December the United States Department of Agriculture officially re-defined federally inspected ham as a food that may be diluted with water." This order, issued without public hearing and without public record, became law when it was published in the *Federal Register* that day. Since then it has been lawful for meat packers, under Federal Meat Inspection, to charge ham prices for water, and to do it without informing customers of that change in the product they buy.*

MORAL LEADERSHIP IN QUESTION

When there is an absence of honesty and moral integrity in government there is bound to follow a weakening of the moral fiber in the citizenry. If the pumping of water into hams is allowed by government agencies with or without informing the consumers that when they buy ham they are paying "ham prices" for common water, is not that dishonesty?

If governmental agencies can do these things is it any wonder that some citizens become specialists in the dishonest handling of their tax reports, and other business affairs? We are more convinced than ever that candidates running for office should have their histories published, so that we

---

* A more recent edict has required that the words "water added" be placed on all such hams.

may have a better idea of the type of men and women we are asked to vote into office.

We sorely need men today of the unimpeachable integrity of Abraham Lincoln, who said: "You may burn my body to ashes and scatter them to the four winds of heaven; you may drag my soul down to the regions of darkness and despair to be tormented forever; but you will not get me to support a measure that I believe to be wrong." God give us more such today. There can never be a moral breakdown in government, in the state, in the community, nor in the home, when every citizen "wears integrity as his coat of mail," and when righteousness is worn as a breastplate.

Faith is the cement that holds integrity as the keystone of the arch of all American freedoms. I use other words: righteousness, honesty, virtue—these are all the fruits of faith. When men truly trust in God they are bound to produce a life of integrity and uprightness. Integrity is more than a gardenia worn in the lapel of the coat, which withers soon after it is cut. Integrity is the spine of the human soul and the body-politic, without which neither men nor women can march upright along the highways of human relations.

This is where we believe Dr. Moffatt's translation of *Ephesians 6:14* is inspiring. The breastplate covers the chest only. Paul evidently expected the Christian never to turn his back on the enemy, but always to move steadily forward in life's conflict.

Paul is right, and the translation true: "Wear integrity as a coat of mail." There is nothing for any man to fear when he is clothed in that armor.

We need, therefore, to cultivate faith in God. "In God

we (must) trust." Just in proportion to our trust in God will be the security of our spiritual, social, economic and human relations. We can keep our integrity intact by cultivating our trust in God and by having our intelligence and wills dedicated to keeping America Christian in spirit and ethics.

Therefore, "stand your ground, having tightened the belt of truth around your loins, having put on integrity as your coat of mail, stand with moral rectitude in the presence of God. Have your feet shod with the preparation of the gospel of peace. Lift over all the shield of faith upon which you can quench all the missiles of the wicked one. Take the helmet of salvation and the sword of the Spirit which is the Word of God. Pray at all times. Keep alert and watch with strong purpose and perseverance; and the love of God will garrison you and keep you in every conflict with evil."

Remember, "the integrity of the upright shall guide them, the perverseness of the transgressors shall destroy them." Therefore, let us wear integrity as our armor.

3

The Enemy Within

Ill fares the land to hastening ills a prey,
When wealth accumulates and men decay.

—*Oliver Goldsmith*

OUR TIMES are out of joint. Many cogs have slipped in the American machinery of life. A question that is being asked more today than at any time in our history is—"what is the matter with our world, our American society?"— Something is wrong. It is not necessary to review the items that are sensationally dealt with by newspaper correspondents, magazine editors, news commentators. We all know that conditions are not as they should be. We have been kept so long on the suspense line that our poise and character as a people are endangered. We can lose our balance.

While traveling by train and plane recently, I began to study American life today by reading magazines, newspapers, special reports, the *Congressional Record*, and a variety of social, economic, and religious papers, and I found that all raise the same questions in one way or another. Is there a decline of morals in America? What is wrong in city, state, and national government? What is happening to the American way of life in general?

Out of these studies, I attempted a diagnosis of individual and national symptoms. I found a striking and disturbing parallelism between individual diseases and the ills that afflict American life.

A STEADY SUBSIDENCE IN VALUES

One thing that gripped me is that the worst enemies to our American way of life work secretly and are not detected until almost irreparable damage is done. All disease germs work silently, and often are not suspected or discovered until they have broken down the cell tissues; then the body must have heroic treatment. These germs work like termites in wood buildings. Unless experts make frequent and thorough examinations the termites are unsuspected until they have eaten out the heart of the wood girders and then, under strain or pressure, the building falls. Just so with the enemies of the American way of life.

My study convinces me that we are afflicted by high blood pressure produced by national tensions. We are in danger of becoming a neurotic people. When the blood pressure is too high, giddiness and other symptoms arise. There is danger of apoplexy. In every phase of our American life there are evidences of tension and pressures which have disastrous effects. In spite of unprecedented leisure time, involvements multiply. The average business man has to rush from one engagement to another. Competition in both domestic and international affairs makes for a constant increase of pressure. Tensions and frustrations multiply until thousands of citizens drop in their tracks through heart attacks. There is so little time for quiet reflection. The rapid pace of life unfits even a religious man for prayer and mediation. Joyous companionship within families is increasingly impractical. This generation of Americans, it seems, simply does not know how to relax.

We also have a high-pressure psychology. Its deadening effect is felt in business, society, politics, and even religion. Those who have particularly exploited the materialistic dialectic of Communism have pushed this pressure to the limit. They have forced the world into a mad race for atomic bombs and nuclear missiles despite their current smugness about having "initiated" the A-Ban Treaty, whose ratification the Western World regards with mixed emotions. Communist threats, chicanery, treachery, deception, all place America and her allies under terrific pressure to be ready for any emergency.

This pressure is also felt in education, where shortcuts have been almost the policy of the day. We mass produce even in our schools. For what? Values of manhood and womanhood are in danger of being lost. Government, business, banks, even labor, think of individuals as numbers, rather than as persons made in the image of God.

The other day I went into a bank and asked for some information. The clerk asked, "What is your number?"— not "What is your name?"

Communist materialism has infiltrated the American system more than is evident at first glance.

Money is minted manhood and has some sacredness to it. Money is congealed character. Cash is coined blood. He who wastes money wastes our country's life. Money is not bad, it is good. Jesus constantly spoke about its value in his parables. But money should never be made to misrepresent the men who make it.

Our American people are our greatest wealth. Only personality can protest or encourage effectively. Today's humanity is being pressured into a mass mechanism by godless materialism, by selfish manipulation and self-willed manipulators. Money is not our god, it is our means for our way of living. There is no substitute for being alive as living personalities with rights as free individuals. This is the image of American manhood and womanhood at its best. Such are not blest by being pressured to the nervous and emotional breaking point.

FALSE VALUES

Also, false values are driving too many people to drink, to narcotics, to soporific pills of one kind or another. Last year hundreds of tons of tranquillizing and sleeping pills were consumed by Americans to quiet their nerves and induce the illusion of restful sleep. The mounting pressures, tensions, and frustrations which more and more characterize American life are creating a mental and moral dizziness. Something is sure to break unless we return to sanity, to moral and spiritual stability. The Bible says, "In quietness and confidence is your strength." We need to take time out to acquire some quietness, some renewed confidence and sanity.

U. S. News & World Report for May 21, 1962, featured a discussion of moral collapse as expressed in crimes of violence and sex extravagances. But these are only two of its manifestations. Contributory to moral collapse are the conditions that destroy self-control, self-discipline, mental, physical and spiritual creative power. These conditions grow directly out of the pressures which first create a national nervousness and a consequent desire to escape.

The route of escape does not lie in the craze for speed, the insatiable lust after narcotics, the appetite for liquor, the demand for thrills. The only deliverance is found in our Lord Jesus Christ. He is our answer. He can and does stabilize the soul. When the disciples were on the sea and in great trouble because of a storm, they received Christ into their ship and, the Scriptures say, "Immediately the ship was at the land whither they went" (*John 6:21*). Americans need this stabilizing power of Christ, Who is the answer to our nervous disorders.

DECLINE OF RESPONSIBILITY

In diagnosing what is the matter with America and with the world, I have also found evidence of arteriosclerosis—hardening of the arteries. Blood pressure has a large part to play in this condition. The patient may become insensitive to touch and the brain may become afflicted. Usually the condition of hardening of the arteries is caused by over-eating, overdrinking, and general immoderation. This is a serious condition throughout American life, affecting both young and old. The symptoms nearly always end in the impairment of the power of attention or concentration, consequently of sound judgment.

As we review the present condition of American life there seems to be a definite hardening of the moral and spiritual arteries impeding healthy circulation. This comes out prominently in a declining sense of responsibility. People do not seem to care what is to become of their country. They can be vociferous in their complaints about politicians, but silent when called upon to elect the right men and women to political offices. They seem insensible to their obligations as citizens. Such people contribute, whether they mean to or not, to the growth of atheistic Communism and the ultimate downfall of their native land.

Likewise, the hardening of the moral and spiritual arteries is expressed in the indifference, lethargy, and apathy toward the good, the wholesome, and the right. Too many people profess a form of Americanism, but deny the power thereof by complete indifference to any real or imagined evil in their community. Paul the apostle, spoke of people becoming so indifferent to righteousness that they were "insensible to God"—to good, and to truth.

Here is the real danger which faces us today. This insensibility is seen in thousands of flagrant cases of ingratitude to God and the American way of life. "They have eyes but they see not, ears have they but they hear not, neither do they understand." This way leads to paralysis and death.

NATIONS DO DIE

Remember, nations do die! History was written in the cemetery of nations. Like individuals, nations are born, have their youth, pass through young adulthood, and then to old age and death. The spade of the archeologist has uncovered the story of an era when Egypt controlled the then known world; nevertheless her sun has set. The Israelitish kingdom gave the world some of its greatest literature and its best moral code; yet she is buried with Nineveh and Tyre. Greece and Athens are gone. The Roman Empire that once stretched from the Sahara to the English Channel and from the Euphrates to the Alps—then the whole world, is "buried in the dust, its glory dead."

Across this scene of desolation the voice of the prophet cries, "The nation that forgets God shall perish. If you will hear my voice and harden not your hearts" then you shall live.

The cure of our national diseases is found (a) in a reactivated faith in God, and (b) in a new self-discipline that can help all of us, from the President down to the humblest citizen, to turn from our wicked ways to a living trust in God. For the Bible is right when it says, "Except you repent, you shall all likewise perish."

Of what shall we repent? Of our sins of indifference and unconcern, of our lust for power, of selfish anxiety on our own behalf without regard for others, of allowing ourselves to become victims of greed, moral laxity, materialism and godlessness. How can we repent? By inviting Christ into our hearts and lives as our Great Physician and personal and national stabilizer; "in quietness and in confidence," wherein lies our strength.

4

Keep Freedom's Holy Light Shining

Freedom has a thousand charms to show that slaves,
howe'er contented, never know.

—*William Cowper*

THE U.S. STATE DEPARTMENT has indicated that
since the beginning of World War II, more than forty
countries in Asia and Africa, with an aggregate population
of 713 million people, have arisen from colonial or de-
pendent status to nationhood. In the same period Communism has extended its rule over more than fourteen
countries, or divisions of them, with a total population of
809 millions. "In each case, this had been accomplished by
the use of force, not through democratic processes."

Our world has been seeing "freedom's holy light" ex-
tinguished in many unhappy areas. Atheistic Communist
leaders are still using force and violence in various parts of
the world to destroy freedom for their own imperialistic
crusade.

I can never forget the thrill I enjoyed when, as an immigrant, our ship passed the Statue of Liberty with her light shining in the darkness, the true symbol of freedom! On that ship I dedicated my life to the task of keeping freedom's "holy light" shining.

A little girl coming to America, when she saw the Statue of Liberty, with the lighted torch in its hand, said to her father, "Daddy, somebody should help that lady hold that light because her hand must get tired." Indeed, somebody must help. That somebody is you and I.

Freedom is "a light that lights every man coming into the world," because God is light and truth and the author of freedom. God being truth and light, therefore, freedom is an inalienable right of every man and woman the world over.

TOLERANCE NOT FREEDOM

History proves that Americans have been, and still are, the champions of freedom. But there is and always has been a difference between freedom and tolerance.

Tolerance is not synonymous with freedom. Tolerance is limited. Freedom is universal. Tolerance is restricted. Freedom is an inalienable right. For example, freedom of conscience is no matter of tolerance. Freedom is a blessing bestowed by God upon men to be enjoyed everywhere. Freedom of speech, freedom to worship according to the dictates of one's own conscience, are not things to be granted by some overlord or tyrant. These are blessings and privileges divinely bestowed just as are the individual's sacred rights to life, liberty and the pursuit of happiness.

Tolerance suggests *permission* granted by a majority or

by some authoritarian, despotic group or person, which may be revoked at their pleasure. Freedom is the "grant deed" to every individual. Americans believe that the minority has the same right as the majority to full freedom to worship, to work, to assemble, to protest or to approve; freedom of speech, and freedom to differ without resort to violence. *These freedoms are the rightful heritage of the weak as well as the powerful.*

In the educational area, academies, colleges and universities become the custodians and exponents of freedom. It is their inescapable duty to help all students to know what freedom is, what freedom has done for their country, what is the cost of maintaining freedom. Our educational institutions are obligated to inspire the students to keep freedom's holy light burning. If we fail to keep freedom alive and vigorous we may someday be the victims of a tyranny more powerful than we can resist. Tolerance may be good, but it is not good enough for Americans.

UPHOLD THE TRUTH

Freedom and truth cannot be separated without endangering both. There can be no "freedom's holy light" without truth. Wherever truth is spurned, or falsified, or withheld, freedom cannot survive.

Our Founding Fathers knew this. They knew that government eventually fails when despots, unprincipled men, kings, or potentates twist the truth or withhold it from the people; or deny the truth. So long as tyrants rule they enslave people, confiscate their property, throw them in jail, or murder them by the firing squad, should they dare to protest.

Our Founding Fathers were essentially men of truth. Therefore, they built schools and colleges to train future Americans in truth, as they found it, in every area of life and knowledge. The first colleges were founded by ministers of the gospel so that youth might be given a sense of purpose in life. They meant to inspire a passion for true freedom for all Americans, having experienced mental, spiritual and physical oppression themselves.

The true test of education is: Does it give all available facts and general knowledge that will inspire in the student a realization that God has a purpose for each life? But it is even more important to help the student to know how to use that knowledge for the betterment and freedom of mankind. Does the student possess the mental, moral and spiritual values that help him to be impervious to lower motives, and make him invincible in character? Does education today assist the student to develop a keen sense of right and wrong, of honor and integrity, and give him an exemplification of the responsibility of freedom? Does education give a youth control of himself?

From our observation, current American education needs a boost in spiritual and moral qualities. Our moral and spiritual development have not kept pace with the tremendous materialistic and scientific advancements. We have been making sixteen-cylinder Cadillac brains but connecting them up with Volkswagen brakes. Freedom's holy light has been dimmed by our nation's increased lawlessness and violence.

When attending a conference in New York I read of a school teacher who had been arrested for stealing trinkets from a department store. The judge said, "I am sad to have to send you to jail for stealing. Do you not know the difference from right and wrong? Do you not know you should not steal?" The teacher replied amazingly, "Your honor, those things don't bother me. The only thing that bothers me is—I was caught."

ETHICAL CONFUSION

Is it not the case that in the lack of emphasis on truth and honor is found much of our present social, political, economic and religious confusion? Freedom does not give any man or nation the right to lie, to deceive, to steal, or to use violence to achieve their ends.

This is one trouble with our world. The disarmament question refuses solution for the absence of mutual honor; the lack of honesty, integrity and truth. We are faced with the ethical unreliability of atheistic Communism, which evidently does not want honest inspection; therefore will not join us in the pursuit of peace. Freedom's holy light can only shine where there is integrity and truth. This is just what the Man of Nazareth meant when he declared, "Men love darkness rather than light because their deeds are evil." Without the oil of truth the light of freedom dies out.

TRUTH STEMS FROM GOD

Truth is not easy to define. However, truth can be expressed in at least two ways. There is universal or absolute truth, such as "the God of truth" (*Deuteronomy 32:4*) and also expressed by Jesus Christ (*John 14:6*). Jesus not only revealed the truth, but also brought us the power to realize the truth. Absolute or universal truth is clear as crystal. It is the unvarnished, undiluted, unadulterated presentation of veritable facts, wherever found. Truth reveals everything to the naked eye; it is the microscope of exactitude.

Relative truth, on the other hand, is an accommodation, modified by knowledge or lack of knowledge and by experience or by all of them. Thus truth to one person may not be truth to another in this sense, no matter how honest or dishonest each may be. Thus we may get limited truth, truth withheld, or half-truth. Partial truth may be a dangerous weapon to deceive, divide, and even destroy when it is used by knaves or experts.

Absolute truth demands knowledge, experience, faith, patience, discernment, integrity. Relative truth may be warped, distorted, perverted by tricky terminology, and even twisted by misusing the art of voice modulation. There can be the premeditated intent to deceive, but *when truth is twisted it becomes a lie.*

Our academies, colleges and universities must, therefore, be committed to the task of helping students to discover the truth and to make that truth available to them. Truth mishandled means the thwarting of justice, the despoiling of the highest nurture.

When all our public officials, statesmen, businessmen know the truth, affirm and practice it, they will lift business, commerce, labor, industry, politics, international diplomacy out of distrust, falsification and chicanery. Let us never forget the words of Jesus, "You shall know the truth and the truth shall make you free."

TRUTH IN CONFLICT

Withholding the truth with deliberate deception has marked the arena where atheistic Communism and Christian democracy come into conflict. Lenin, the high priest of Communism, says, "A Communist must be prepared to make every sacrifice, if necessary, even to resort to schemes and stratagems, employ illegitimate methods, conceal the truth, in order to get into trade unions, stay there, and conduct the revolutionary work within."

There we have it—"to withhold the truth, to conceal the truth." Thus, through this diabolical device, they would destroy our freedoms if they could. The conflict between the darkness of evil and the light of truth is really at the core of our world's "cold war." It is again the ancient struggle:

> Truth forever on the scaffold,
> Wrong forever on the throne.
> But that scaffold sways the future,
> And behind the dim unknown standeth God
> Within the shadows, keeping watch above His own.

Truth will win if we are courageous and enthusiastic enough to make it work in all of our American life.

We need to be challenged to an almost fanatical enthusiasm for truth, that will more than match the fanaticism of Communism, so as to keep freedom's holy light burning on America's altars. It is a light that must never be allowed to go out.

5

Faith That
Made America Free

America—the home of freedom, the hope of the
down-trodden and oppressed among the nations of
the earth.

—*Daniel Webster*

AMERICA HAS BEEN the champion of freedom not
only for herself but for the world. This ideal is derived
from the faith that prevails in the hearts of the people.

Suspicion and doubt are not constructive. It is certain
that doubters did not set America free nor did doubt bring
freedom and courage to the American soul. There was no
doubt in the mind of Jesus when He said, "All things are
possible to him who believes." It is that kind of faith that
liberates and builds.

It is good sometimes to go back in history and study
great movements and the men who inspired those movements. We hear a lot about "The Big Four" nations of our

day. But "The Big Four" of early American history were men: Washington, Jefferson, Franklin and John Adams.

TRUTH BRINGS STABILITY

These men all were manifestly convinced that Jesus was right when He said, "You shall know the truth and the truth shall make you free." To them truth was, the foundation of all freedom. They knew that lies and deception are the shifting sands of political chicanery. There can never be a stable form of civilization that is built on deception and untruths. Trust and confidence are fundamental to a stabilized form of government and to a growing brotherly civilization. Washington, Franklin, Jefferson and Adams established freedom under the government of God.

In the *Dissertation*, John Adams declared:

Liberty must, at all hazards, be supported. We have a right to it from the Maker . . . rulers are no more than attorneys, agents, and trustees of the people.

Later, Adams wrote:

I would ask by what law the (English) Parliament has authority over America? By the law of God it has none . . . by the law of nature and nations it has none.

Adams wrote those words before the First Congress of the United States was organized. It took courage to do it. But he was a man of faith in God, in right, and believed that right was mightier than political power. He had faith in himself. But from that day on he was a marked man. It is evident from all he wrote that John Adams believed he was in the hands of God in the forward movement toward the establishment of the United States of America.

George Washington was a family man. He was not a man of war. He loved his family and his farm and longed to stay with them. But when there seemed to be a divine call to liberate his nation, he put God and his country first. He was convinced that no man can be truly a man, at his best, unless or until he is free. We cannot study with an open mind the life, works and actions of Washington without being convinced that his true greatness came through his faith in God. George Washington drove from his beloved Mount Vernon each Sunday to church where he was a vestryman. He was a man of prayer. His private secretary and nephew, Robert Lewis, said of him:

I accidentally witnessed Washington's private devotions in his library, both morning and evening. On occasions, I saw him in a kneeling posture, with a Bible open before him. I believe such to have been his daily practice.

Such active, simple faith in divine providence as was Washington's made him a man of high integrity; honest, selfless, just, and sound in family life. Washington, Adams, and Franklin all looked ahead. Theirs was not a backward faith but a forward-looking one.

FAITH IN GOD AND MAN

Such faith means assurance, trust, confidence in God. In the darkest days of the Revolution our Founding Fathers were not pessimists. Faith masters pessimism. The doubters are the pessimists. Men of faith hold on to that "invisible something" that is rewarding and enduring. In those early days these men had reason to question the whole existing order, but they did not stop at questioning; they had a faith in God, and with it a longing to see the triumph of right, so they held tenaciously to their belief in the ultimate triumph of their cause.

Many men confronted with the dire circumstances our Founding Fathers faced would have given up in despair. But not these men! Their foundation was steadfast because their faith was in the unshakable God.

This kind of faith is deeply religious and therefore is identical and continuous in quality with the faith they employed every day. It is faith in God that gives assurance and stability. "This is the victory that overcomes the world," says the word of God, "even our faith."

This is the faith that helped George Washington to do his best. Read again these words which Washington spoke to a Hebrew congregation in Savannah May, 1790:

May the same working-day Deity who, long since delivering the Hebrews from their Egyptian oppressors, planted them in the promised land—whose providential agency has lately been conspicuous in establishing these United States as an independent nation—still continue to water them with the dews of Heaven and make them the inhabitants of every denomination participating in the temporal and spiritual blessings of that people whose God is Jehovah.

Our American citizens need to be discriminating in evaluating glib speeches by politicians who make cheap promises and forget them when they are elected. We need men of heart and of courage, men of unfailing honesty and high integrity; men who are selfless for the sake of making America just what our Founding Fathers gave themselves to make it, and what we feel God wants America to be. We need men of the conviction and dedication of John Adams who, in his defense of the Declaration of Independence said:

Sir, before God, I believe the hour has come. My judgment approves this measure and my whole heart is in it. All that I have, and all that I am, and all that I hope, in this life, I am now ready here to stake upon it: and I leave off as I began, that live or die, survive or perish, I am for the Declaration. It is my living sentiment, and by the blessing of God it shall be my dying sentiment. Independence now, and independence forever.

Too often we read newspaper accounts of investigations going on from the city, county, state to federal levels, of dishonest transactions, all involving men who have no vital faith in God, in right, in their constituencies, or in the country. Therefore, we have a right to ask every candidate for political office at any level what he believes concerning American standards and liberties; ideals which concern the freedom of speech, freedom of worship, human rights, and concerning their attitudes toward the separation of church and state. Citizens have a right to know what our public servants believe and no one should be afraid to tell the citizenry what are his religious affiliations and whether or not he is dedicated to the American free enterprise way of life. We need to be represented by men of faith and righteous character.

THE FAITH THAT PRESERVES

Faith in God is the best safeguard for freedom of religion, of speech, of the press and all the other freedoms. Today we need a rebirth of the same faith that motivated John Adams, George Washington, Thomas Jefferson, Benjamin Franklin and others throughout all of the areas of American life. When we as Americans, with open mind, search for the truth, obtain the truth, act upon the truth, and keep a lively trust in God, we will enthusiastically exercise our citizenship obligations and keep America true to its ideals.

The faith that brought our freedoms to America must be kept alive at all costs. This faith will be actively preserved only when American citizens practice it in everyday living and duties—in the home, in the school, the church, the community, and the nation.

The Bible is the source-book for freedom lovers and freedom thinkers. Our Lord has given us the prescription, in opening the way to a comprehensive knowledge of the truth. This means that in our communities we must perpetually have free libraries, free schools, free churches, free institutions and the free ballot. Where these things are encouraged we find the great freedoms still alive.

The atheistic Communist governments are biased against the truth. Therefore they will not let their people be free to express themselves. They are not allowed the freedom to speak as they may inwardly feel. Thus, millions of sincere people, who desire the freedoms we enjoy, are kept in mental and some in physical slavery.

When enough men know the truth, they will also know the blessings and beauty of liberty. This was the burden of Julia Ward Howe when she wrote:

> In the beauty of the lilies Christ was born across the sea
> With a glory in his bosom that transfigures you and me.
> As He died to make men holy, let us live to keep men free!
> While God is marching on!

In this faith let us live, and let us die, if need be, for the glory of God and the welfare of humanity.

6

The Patriotism of Peace

Peace does not mean the end of all our striving;
Joy does not mean the drying of our tears
Peace is the power that comes to souls arriving
Up to the light where God Himself appears.
—*G. A. Studdert-Kennedy*

PATRIOTISM IS INFINITELY more than the blowing of tin horns, the waving of flags and martial parades on the Fourth of July, or standing at salute when the Star Spangled Banner passes by. These may be manifestations of our patriotism. But patriotism and militarism are not synonymous. Patriotism is idealistic and spiritual. History shows that militarism is materialistic and thrives on suspicion, half-truths, and intrigue. Patriotism deals with principles, righteousness, national honor. Truly it is love for one's country—but love of country at its very best.

To most of us patriotism and religion are inseparable. While they are not the same, there can be no true patriotism without religion and no true religion without real patriotism. Jesus recognized this when He said, "Render to

Caesar the things that are Caesar's, and to God the things that are God's."

Patriotism is natural to thoughtful citizens. Sir Walter Scott meant this when he wrote,

> Breathes there the man with soul so dead
> Who never to himself hath said
> This is my own, my native land!

Patriotism is essential to national integration and social protection. It is concerned with social, moral, economic, spiritual—yes, with all human relationships, as well as with missiles. It seems more difficult to stir patriotic endeavor in time of peace than in war. Love of country appears to be more evident when men are hating another country. There certainly is more patriotic excitement in wartime than in peace. In peace-time there is little of the spectacular; no tramp, tramp of soldiers to the music of military bands, no bidding of farewells, few medals for heroic service. Nevertheless, peace does challenge men to slow, painstaking, honest construction in the building of a nation, a people, a civilization on high humanitarian principles.

LIVING FOR PEACE

It is often harder and takes more courage to live exemplarily for one's country than to die gallantly for it. The patriotism of peace is very exacting for the lover of freedom.

This we believe: that every citizen, native-born or naturalized, must repudiate the culture, traditions, and ideology of other lands when these conflict with the ideals and

Christian spirit of America. There can be no "split loyalty" in true American patriotism, as the laws concerning naturalization declare. Moreover, there can be no "hyphenated" Americans so far as true American citizenship is concerned. On this, the naturalization oaths are explicit. Yet tens of thousands of Americans are ignorant of the laws and conditions of naturalization, which govern both native-born and foreign-born Americans.

WHAT NATURALIZATION MEANS

When I became an American citizen, I had to reside in the United States at least five years before making final application for citizenship. I then had to make a declaration of intention, stating that I intended to become a citizen of the United States, and at the end of seven years I applied to a United States District Court for citizenship. Before my citizenship papers were granted I had to pass a searching examination on the U. S. Constitution; some phases of American history, traditions of the flag, and other civic matters.

This may now be done by attending schools for naturalization or by taking an examination before a U. S. District Court examiner when no school of naturalization is held. If the candidate is successful, he then is asked to forswear "all allegiance to every foreign king, prince, potentate, or ruler, especially of king, or prince, or potentate so-and-so of whom he is now subject." He then swears allegiance to the flag of our nation and "to uphold and defend the Constitution of the United States of America." He is required to sign his oath of allegiance to the Constitution of the United States, and the judge declares him an American citizen with all the rights and privileges and responsibilities of citizenship.

The reason for all this is to impress upon the candidate that he cannot be a citizen of two countries at the same time. When one surrenders to this exacting ordeal of forswearing all allegiance to every foreign king, potentate, prince, or ruler, he cuts loose from every other country in everything that conflicts with his obligations to the United States. This surrender is evidence of a new birth, a new loyalty, and a new life. The center of his civic life changes. So far as he is concerned, he now believes that he can serve his God and humanity most completely by committing himself to the land of his adoption. He is an American, without a hyphen.

Then, as an American citizen, he is obligated to honor American institutions, uphold American ideals, obey the laws of the land and serve his country to the fullest extent of his ability. If at any time he believes the laws should be changed, he will seek those changes in the proper manner provided by the Constitution and the Government.

A SACRED OBLIGATION

General Washington, America's first president, declared his own convictions in his Farewell Address:

> This Government, the offspring of your own choice, uninfluenced and unawed, adopted upon full investigation and mature deliberation, completely free in its principles . . . has a just claim to your confidence and your support. Respect for authority, compliance

with its laws, acquiescence in its measures, are duties enjoined by the fundamental maxims of true liberty. The basis of our political system is the right of the people to make and to alter their Constitution or Governments. But the Constitution which at any time exists, till changed by explicit and authentic act of the people, is sacredly obligatory upon all.

The true patriot is an enthusiastically obedient citizen who sets an example of devotion and unselfish service to God, his country and the world.

Patriotism demands respect, not ridicule; fealty, not sedition; devotion, not alienation. Patriotism calls for fidelity to the moral and spiritual as well as to the economic and political welfare of the citizenry.

Patriotism expresses a positive, aggressive action against social evils. It is an antidote against the immoral and political poisons that would infect the body politic. One who betrays a public trust in time of peace is just as truly a traitor as one who betrays his country in time of war. The man or woman who seeks to undermine the foundations of democracy, liberty, justice, and righteousness is a real traitor no matter how much he may shout about the "dear old flag."

The true patriot is one who serves his country and his God by having a stainless character, a faultless integrity, and a deathless devotion to truth, honor, freedom, and to God. This patriotism goes wherever the patriot goes. "When in Rome do as the Romans do" is not the patriot's slogan, particularly when it means the repudiation of his country's institutions, traditions, and ideals. Wherever he goes the free patriot always remembers that the privileges of the American free-enterprise way of life is the best for him. He wishes to be an example and to share it with others who know the inspiration of independence. He will refuse to lower his moral, spiritual and patriotic standards.

I was aboard an American liner crossing the Atlantic after World War I. In the hold of the ship were scores of bodies of American soldiers who had given their lives on the fields of France. The ship was draped in black, and flags were flying at half mast. A memorial service was held on Sunday. But almost immediately after the service passengers went down to the gambling tables. A jazz band struck up and people crowded into the ballroom to dance to the wail of the saxophone. Yes—

> The cymbals crash and the dancers stalk
> With their long silk stockings and
>   arms of chalk,
> With butterfly skirts and white breasts
>   bare—
> With the spirits of dead soldiers
>   watching there.

The whole thing seemed to me an ironic portrayal of so-called patriotism . . . cheap Americanism dancing on its own coffin.

NEED FOR REVERENCE

Contrast that attitude with the spirit, life, and example of men like George Washington on his knees at Valley Forge; Abraham Lincoln kneeling in the White House and Theodore Roosevelt speaking about the Bible before thousands of University of California students in the Greek Theatre.

The patriotic American's regard for human personality and freedom makes him respect the symbols of governmental authority. To him the flag is more than a piece of colored bunting. It represents American ideals, sacrifices, spirit and life. The colors in it are just right; the red of genuine sacrificial service, the white of pure motives and clean living, and the blue of dynamic loyalty to God and country and the high principles for which the flag stands.

True patriotism calls for unreserved, wholehearted, enthusiastic allegiance. Jesus said, "No man can serve two masters; for either he will hate the one and love the other." It is not true patriotism when a man constantly measures America in the light of the policies of the nation from which he comes, or of any other nation, and holds America in ridicule or even in contempt. Mixed allegiance is incompatible with honest patriotism. Office seekers who appeal to groups as Negro-Americans, Irish-Americans, Italian-Americans, and such, are not behaving as patriots. They tend to be divisives and subversive of our country's unity and freedom.

True patriotism is based on a living faith in a benevolent God. From the day when John Robinson read the Scriptures on the rocky shores of New England after the Pilgrims had assembled from the "Mayflower," to the time when President Eisenhower prayed his own written prayer at his inauguration, religion has inspired and energized true patriotism in America. Religious faith shaped the concept of the state for the Pilgrims.

The Preamble of the Constitution of the American Legion recognizes that patriotism and religion are indissolubly bound up together. After the declaration, "For God and country," follows a description of the aims of the true patriot. That is why American Legionnaires are concerned with the rights of individuals, the rights of the minority as well as of the majority.

Freedom is the jewel that must be maintained in its completeness. There are, however, some rules governing freedom. Freedom of speech, worship, the press, of assembly —all presuppose that these will never be used for violent and destructive ends. Like the airplane, patriotism needs the stabilizer; as the locomotive needs the governor; as the ship needs the rudder. It seeks to establish a happy society and a strong nation because it endeavors to produce the satisfied man. No man can be truly happy unless and until he is free.

This I believe, as did John Robinson when he read from the Bible "I will make thee a great nation and I will bless thee, and make thy name great, and thou shalt be a blessing: And I will bless them that bless thee, and curse him that curseth thee: and in thee shall all the families of the earth be blessed" (*Genesis 12:2,3*).

No finer thing can we do than to dedicate our lives to the realization of the inalienable rights guaranteed by our American Constitution. Patriotism for peace demands this dedication.

7

The Nausea
of Neutrality

> Because you are lukewarm, and neither cold nor
> hot, I will spew you out of my mouth.
>
> —*Revelation 3 : 16 RSV*

THE BIBLE ENCOURAGES believers to be out and
out, either cold or hot, so that God, our friends, yes, even
our enemies, may know where we stand.

The insipidness of neutrality is responsible for many of
the divisions found within American life today. There are
too many, in places of power and authority, who make
matters worse by trying to be neutral between God and
Khrushchev, between Russia and the United States of
America. The Bible says we should always be ready to give
a reason for the hope we have within us. Our forefathers
gave a reason, unashamed, and under all circumstances, and
on all occasions. Their faith came out of their personal experience. They had felt the heel of the oppressor and the
mailed fist of the tyrant. Out of intolerance and inquisition,

their conviction was born. Most of their world was under dictatorships when they came to this country. History indicates that it was their faith in God, their dedication to freedom, their clear thinking, and hard work that energized their ability to overcome insurmountable difficulties and "bring forth on this continent a new nation under God, conceived in liberty, and dedicated to the service of mankind."

Their faith was more than a passing emotional experience; it made them "Gibraltar-like" personalities. They were men who could match our mountains, because they were men and women of divine conviction, determination, and action. "This one thing I do," was their commitment. They determined to make America something like the kingdom of God on earth.

TO BUILD A NATION, UNDER GOD

Of course, they were human beings and therefore subject to the weaknesses of the flesh. But they were sincere, clear minded, determined, human beings. They had a vision. They were not disobedient to that vision. Courageously, they declared themselves for God's way of life. To them, faith in God was a spiritual dynamic, not a sectarian affair.

Their ideals were Christian. The early charters of the colonies emphasized faith in God, integrity, and liberty. These founders let the world know on whose side they stood, always unashamed.

That was perfectly natural. When anyone commits himself to Christ's way of life, he has to make a decision. The Bible says there is the way that is right and also there is a way that *seems* right. They believed the way under God, guided by God, was the way to follow.

History shows that the majority of them lived in that way, and followed Him who said, "I am the way, the truth and the life."

To build a nation made up of men and women who had the spirit of Christ was their determined goal. It should be ours as well. Jesus Christ is the world's outstanding leader of convictions born of divine knowledge. His convictions motivated Him and energized His decisions. Christ's day demanded men and women who believed they were right, because they were following Him.

With Christ there was only the right and the left. There was no in-between, no middle ground, no neutrality. A man was either for Christ or against Him.

The Bible says there was "a middle wall of partition between us." But it also says, "Christ has broken down that middle wall," so that we are either on God's side or on the side of His great enemy. When the middle wall was broken down, the line was exceedingly fine between left and right, good and evil, life and death. It meant, no one can stand neutral. He is either on one side or the other, on the right or on the left, hot or cold.

A HINDRANCE TO LIFE AND FREEDOM

Let us note some of the declarations in the Bible concerning Christ and neutrality. These should convince any American that there is no neutrality that is not a hindrance to life and freedom, and that does not create nausea in the heart of God.

Jesus said, "I am the light of the world," not "I am an eternal twilight;" "I am the truth," not "the divine equivocator" nor "the political compromiser;" "I am the way," not "the everlasting wanderer."

Jesus said men are either "lost or found," not "in a condition of perpetual bewilderment." He said, "We are saved or lost," not "forever in a state of emotional uncertainty." Jesus said, "We are free men or slaves," "We are at liberty or in chains." He said, "We were dead, but are alive again," not "in a state of universal, perpetual, suspended animation."

He said, "We step out of darkness into light," not "into a perennial spiritual smog." Jesus said, "We travel either to the right or to the left," and not "into a middle ground of neutrality, vagueness and irresolution."

Jesus also cuts clear when He says "No man can serve two masters. Either he will hate the one and love the other; or else he will hold to the one, and despise the other. Ye cannot serve God and mammon."

In all of history no one ever declared himself more positively, or demanded so absolute a commitment and loyalty than did Jesus Christ. Everybody knew where Christ stood on all questions. Moreover they also knew where His disciples stood, because they had to come out and declare themselves. The risen Christ said, "Remember, because you are neither cold nor hot, you nauseate me." Also, "He who is not with me is against me and he who gathers not with me scatters." Of all the words Jesus spoke, none were so sharp, so clear-cut, so final, as these. He divides us into two opposing groups. We are either with Him or against Him.

With Jesus there is no middle ground. To Him we are either cold or hot. We gather with Him or we scatter.

One of the most beautiful descriptions Jesus gave of Himself is implied right in this Scripture. He is the gatherer and He wants us to gather to Him. Christ came to gather together all of His disobedient children into one redeemed family. What are we American fathers doing with our own families? By the sad record of broken families, it seems that millions of fathers and mothers are scattering their families rather than gathering. God save us American parents from being scatterers.

CLEAR CONVICTION NEEDED

There are some people who are pathetically sincere in their neutralism. Nevertheless, that sincerity will not save them or us from the avowed and determined destruction by atheistic Communism. These neutralists know how sensitive real Americans are to any application of force. Americans want to settle their problems in the Christian way of open-sky discussions with people who have integrity, whose word is unimpeachable.

The record of atheistic Communist Russia, in making promises and never keeping their word, is known to everyone who reads and thinks. We know how these Communists exploded immense nuclear bombs during the moratorium agreed upon by Khrushchev, the United States and the Allied nations. Khrushchev "could not wait for further discussions." Remember, America did not explode bombs for war purposes during the agreement.

In the area of bomb testing, America has demanded only

that there be a system of adequate inspection against making bombs and other destructive war machines by every nation. But the Communists say that would be "spying," proving the saying that "The Russian Communists measure others by their own false bushel." They do not mean what they say, so cannot believe what anyone else says. Since they use every available privilege for their spy system, they think other nations will do the same.

Our world needs Americans of the highest integrity and men of the noblest dedication to God and our beloved country. America should be first in our thinking, and then our goal should be to help make the whole world free under "the liberty we have in Christ."

When Christ says, "He who is not with me is against me," this is His condemnation of neutrality. Peter was neutral when the maids came to Him in the patio near the Judgment Hall. Judas was neutral at the Last Supper, but both of them played into the hands of Christ's enemies. Neutralism is self-centeredism. The neutral person does not want to be disturbed. He is absorbed in his own selfish world. This was expressed in a story told by Jim Backus. During a terrible fire in California some years ago, at the height of the tragedy, a group of the refugees gathered on the Bel Air golf course for safety. While watching their homes going up in flames with all of their personal effects, they were suddenly forced to scatter by a golf ball, as a golf foursome approached. One of the golfers shouted to a woman who was weeping because her home was in flames. "Woman, stop that crying while I'm putting."

There is a good description of the neutralist. He cares about no one but himself and his own "putting"; seems interested only in keeping on "putting" while the world burns. Concern over world tragedy might affect his pleasure. He despises anyone who makes him think.

A minister, to illustrate the evils of Russian Communism, was quoting a declaration of hate by a Party member, when a visitor heard a member of the church say, "There you are. He's talking about Communism again. Why doesn't he preach the Gospel?"

God has something to say about such: "Son of man, I have made thee a watchman . . . hear the word at my mouth. . . . If thou warn the wicked, and he turn not from his wickedness, nor from his wicked way, he shall die in his iniquity; but thou hast delivered thy soul. . . . Nevertheless, if thou warn the righteous man, that the righteous sin not, and he doth not sin, he shall surely live, because he is warned; also thou hast delivered thy soul."

God wants all of us to be awake to evil, to forsake it, and to turn in trust to Him and follow His way and do His will.

We Americans need to be convicted of some of the clearcut principles for which America stands in this world. Conviction masters neutrality. Faith in God is something we can express and let the world know where we stand. People have a right to know where we stand, whether for God or against Him, whether for America or against America, whether we gather for Christ or scatter abroad, whether we are cold or hot.

We can answer God's call right now with the words of

the Prophet Isaiah, "Here am I, Lord. Send me" (*Isaiah 6:1-8*).

[This message was printed in the May, 1964 issue of *The Christian Herald* and is here reproduced with their consent.]

8

If Christ Be Not Risen

. . . if Christ be not risen, then is our preaching vain; and your faith is also vain . . . You are still in your sins.

—I Corinthians, 15 : 14-17

IF CHRIST IS NOT RAISED from the dead, then the whole of the Christian faith is shattered. If Christ is not raised from the dead, then Christianity is folly and the many years of preaching of thousands of ministers, the preaching of the disciples, the ministers, priests, evangelists, and Christian laymen, for the past nearly 2,000 years, has all been vain—that is, useless—and the gospel we have preached for many years is foolishness. Paul says, "If Christ be not risen, then you are still in your sins." That means, no matter how often you and I have confessed our sins to God, if Christ is not risen, then we are still unforgiven, and lost to holiness, lost to heaven, and lost to God.

But thanks be unto God, "Now, is Christ risen from the dead and has become the first fruit of them that slept." Because Christ is risen, therefore, Christ shall reign, be-

cause He must reign until He has put all His enemies under His feet, and the last enemy to be destroyed is death.

A POWER IN THIS WORLD

The resurrection of Christ is the cardinal miracle of the
world, and of the ages. According to the Apostle John,
"Many other miracles did Jesus which are not written in
this book." But no matter if all the miracles had been recorded, they would be utterly void in power to establish
Christ's claims of authority, if He did not rise from the
dead.

Christ did rise from the dead, and the fact of His resurrection will support all the miracles that have been at-
tributed to Him. Jesus is declared "to be the Son of God
with power, according to the spirit of holiness, by the resurrection from the dead" (*Romans 1:3*).

The gospel is not founded on a fake, but upon a fact:
not on a theory, a doctrine, a science, a philosophy, a new
thought, a psychology, or anything other than fact. Our
gospel is founded on the personal resurrection of Jesus
Christ. Nothing less than the fact of Christ's resurrection
will bring comfort and soul satisfaction to men and women
in bereavement and sorrow.

Christ is raised from the dead. Therefore, Christianity has
been endowed with divine power of comfort and mental
and spiritual healing. The resurrection of Christ has made
Christianity the only sympathetic religion that has invaded
our world. We have seen the comforting, steadying, healing power of the gospel of resurrection. It has always
brought assurance and help, no matter how great the bereavement has been.

Those to whom we have brought this gospel of resurrection would never have been helped by the so-called philosophic, pseudopsychological, materialistic, scientific theories that are being peddled from public platforms. When a mother and father have lost a child, they don't want to hear about the circuitous concourse of atoms, or the atheistic Communist's materialistic dialectic.

Tell a broken-hearted mother that her child died because it was not fit to live. Try the doctrine of "the survival of the fittest" on her, and you will not bring any hope or comfort to her. Just tell a wife, whose husband has died after a long life of marital happiness, that it was an economic necessity for him to die, and you will find she will not respond kindly to that sort of sociological twaddle. Nevertheless, we have seen sad hearts calmed, tears assuaged, and souls aglow when we have brought to them the living words of God, "I go to prepare a place for you, and I will come again and receive you unto myself. . . . My peace I leave with you. My peace I give unto you, not as the world giveth, give I unto you. Let not your heart be troubled, neither let it be afraid." "Because I live ye shall live also." There is life in God's word.

The sad and bereaved want to hear most of all a message of hope and assurance, "The Lord is my shepherd; I shall not want. . . . Though I walk through the valley of the shadow of death, I will fear no evil: for thou art with me. . . . Surely goodness and mercy shall follow me all the days of my life: and I shall dwell in the house of the Lord forever."

EVIDENCES OF A LIVING FAITH

There is power in the resurrection. Let us claim it. Then we will understand what Paul spoke about in referring to his experience of Christ's resurrection. It will be Christ, the living Christ, in you the hope of glory. Other religions preach some good things, but they do not give us a conquering Saviour and a living Lord.

The resurrection of Christ, when accepted by living faith, works miracles within us. Take our world as it is today; we are seeing tragic events as well as amazing feats of scientific achievement. Our forebears would have been frightened if they had returned to see on television the successful launching of Colonel Glenn into outer space, and his safe return after a three-time orbit around the earth. We thank God for such achievements. We also know, however, that there is another side of life, where millions of people are living under oppression, and fear, and in slavery. And the foundations of many great institutions, that have brought blessings to mankind, are being shaken, because of a lack of integrity in high places. Truly,

> Our little systems have their day
> They have their day, and cease to be.

IT BRINGS HOPE TO ALL

Nevertheless, the resurrection of Christ brings hope and inspires us with faith to win through. Too often, we cultivate attitudes of gloom, fear, and failure. The power of the resurrection has the dynamic that we all need when we are, as we say, "down in the dumps." The resurrection says to you and me, in our most discouraged moments, "You can win." The resurrection makes hope alive and vital.

One reason why the great oratorio, *The Messiah*, is still challenging millions today, is because it expresses the power of the resurrection, not only as it refers to our omnipotent God in Christ, "That He shall reign forever and ever," but because it came out of the true resurrection experience of Handel the composer. Handel had fought a bitter fight. His health was bad; his one side paralyzed. He seemed hopelessly in debt, and his creditors threatened him with imprisonment. He had reached the bottom.

But, somehow, the gospel of the resurrection of Christ gripped his soul. It gave him strength to hold out a little longer. He gave himself with utter abandon to producing one of the world's great masterpieces. When you hear *The Messiah* again, remember that Handel was passing through what we call "his Good Friday" before he experienced the resurrection. Through the power of the resurrection he won.

If Christ is not risen, then would our hope of life and victory be in vain just as well as our preaching. Therefore, do not give up. Our Lord is saying to all of us under testing, "The resurrection will follow every Good Friday." Believe it.

Here is hope for all America. We, as a great country, are passing through the valley of the shadows. Too many of our politicians think they can solve our troubles by spending money we do not have, by getting more power over individuals as well as over the industries and businesses of the land.

A RENEWAL OF FAITH NEEDED

Christian Americans must renew their faith in the power of the resurrection. God will say, and is now saying to all of us who have committed our lives to Him, "Never give up —don't quit." For remember, "no man having put his hand to the plow and looking back is fit for the kingdom of God."

We Christian men and women must not quit. We should redouble our faith, increase our energies and strengthen our Christian witness. We should be more loyal to our churches, more generous in our Christian giving, more alert to the opportunities for Christian service. The power of the resurrection is felt in every heart that gives Christ full control. We are "passed from death unto life." That is the miracle that can be wrought in every heart and throughout the land today.

If we could help more people to give this power a chance in their lives, we could redeem our land from godless socialism, godless materialism, godless theatricalism. I know some skeptics do not believe that God can work a miracle today. A British worker was asked whether he really believed that Jesus turned water into wine at Cana of Galilee. The young man said, "I don't know about that, but I do know that, in my house, He changed beer into furniture, and whiskey into food and clothing for my wife and kids, and that's miracle enough for me." I, too, have seen that miracle in hundreds of English and American homes. This is the result wrought by the power of Christ's resurrection.

"If Christ be not risen!" "But thanks be unto God who

gives us the victory through our Lord Jesus Christ. Therefore, my beloved brethren be you steadfast, unmovable, always abounding in the work of the Lord forasmuch as you
know, your labor is not in vain in the Lord" (*1 Corinthians
15:58*).

9

Making Pain
into Pearls

> And lest I should be exalted above measure through the abundance of the revelations, there was given to me a thorn in the flesh, the messenger of Satan to buffet me. . . .
>
> —*2 Corinthians 12:7*

SUFFERING IS A GREAT revealer; adversity is a crucible; trouble proves us; trial is a great factor in character building.

It cannot be too often impressed upon us that life's great aim is character building. Not for selfish gain, not for fame, not for money making nor yet for pleasure seeking. God is too great, too benevolent, too progressive to desire for man anything less than the highest possible ideal—the realization of the Kingdom of God on earth through God-like characters; in other words, perfect humanity. He desires a race of perfect personal characters, capable of pure love for each other; capable of keenly discerning God's purposes, of doing His will, of sharing His fellowship and of enjoying his blessedness.

Christ is the architect of character. His specialty is character building. He throws light upon our problem. *Hebrews 2:10* declares, "It became Him (Christ) for whom are all things, and by whom are all things, in bringing many sons unto glory, to make the captain of their salvation perfect through sufferings."

The problem of suffering with its greatest ally, evil, has puzzled the profoundest thinkers. Why do men suffer? Why does a benevolent God permit so much suffering in His world?

SIN'S INFECTIONS BRING PAIN

It is certain there would be no suffering if there had been no sin. But to say all suffering is due to the sufferer's wrong doing, finds no warrant in the Scriptures. There is much suffering, perhaps most of it, which is the result of one's own sin, neglect and wilfullness "Be not deceived; God is not mocked: for whatsoever a man soweth, that shall he also reap. For he that soweth to the flesh shall of the flesh reap corruption . . ." (*Galatians 6:7,8*).

Suffering for one's sin should soften the hardened heart, lead one to repentance, confession and salvation.

1. Suffering is sent as an aid in making character to train the soul in self discipline and self mastery.
2. Suffering aids in subduing the rebellious will. David said: "Before I was afflicted I went astray, but now have I kept Thy word" (*Psalms 119:67*).
3. Pain deepens character. Many a life is shallow and

superficial until it has felt the dredging power of adversity.

4. Some of the most persecuted have become the most virile, the hardiest and most courageous of souls. Character has been strengthened by adversity.

5. Trouble tests the stability of the soul. The exquisite book of Job was evidently given us to prove this truth. Job had committed no special sin, yet he was tested and his character comes out of it beautified and unshaken. "Though He slay me yet will I trust him," he exclaims triumphantly in his trial. "Behold I have refined thee in the furnace of affliction," therefore

> Be patient suffering soul,
> I hear thy cry,
> The trial fires may glow
> But I am nigh.
> I see the gold I must refine
> Until my image upon thee shine.

Adversity comes to all. Do not borrow it. There are plenty of people who will cause you annoyance without your seeking it. But trouble comes to all in its season. What shall we do with it when it comes? That is the question.

THE MAKING OF THE PEARL

Last year I was introduced to the pearl industry of India. It was one of the most interesting experiences of my life. The oyster is a great teacher. The pearl is the glorified crystallization of pain. While the oyster bathes itself in the warm waters of the southern seas, a little uninvited guest enters the oyster's home and takes up residence in its sensitive curtains. The oyster resents the irritation and does its best to eject the intruder. It fails, but it does not despair. Out of its little muscular body it exudes juices and determinedly, and persistently exerts all its powers until the little foreigner has been transmuted into a pearl. Without the suffering the pearl would not be formed; thus pain produces the pearl. The gates of the new Jerusalem are of one pearl, we are told; a significant symbolism, reminding us that through tribulation we enter the Kingdom.

What is the pearl? It is the story of transformed discomfort. It is an aggravation changed into an exaltation. It is an obstacle turned into a benediction. It is darkness changed into radiance, pain into pleasure, failure into success, defeat into victory, trial into triumph, disease into health.

A pearl is the symbol of an experience, of great discomfort translated into beauty. It is a parable of adversity transmuted into Christlikeness by the alchemy of faith, patience, courage and determination. Thus in this symbolic sense pain can be transnatured into the "joy of pearls." That is the parable of the oyster. If the unthinking oyster can make an irritation into a gem of glory, surely man made in the image of God may turn trouble into Godlikeness and annoyance into "pearls for His diadem."

THE SCHOOL OF AFFLICTION

Affliction is the school in which great virtues are acquired and fine characters formed. Spiritual beauty comes often through physical suffering.

No one would surmise from reading the works of Robert Louis Stevenson that he fought for twenty years a grim battle with an insidious disease and that many of his most sparkling paragraphs were composed between spasms of pain and hemorrhages which threatened to carry him off at any moment.

Edward Noyes Westcott, author of that inimitable and cheerful *David Harum* suffered under the stress of endless pain and sorrow until his book was finished, when he yielded to death before he could enjoy the rewards of his heroic efforts.

No one has filled the world with more beautiful songs and spiritual messages than Fanny Crosby, yet she did not see the light of day. Over ten thousand songs of the gospel came from her soul.

Green, the noted historian, was an invalid for years, but he continued at his great work and finished it before disease could kill him. It was by sheer faith and will power that he kept disease from doing its worst until he had dedicated to the English people that history which will make his name famous for generations. "He died learning" was the appropriate epitaph placed upon his tombstone.

There are countless more of these heroic invalids who have filled the world with songs of joy instead of deluging us with wearisome details of their sufferings.

Suffering has also evoked rich music. Schubert claimed that his musical compositions were the product of his genius and his misery. Shelley tells us that the poets learn in suffering what they teach us in song.

HOW WE DEAL WITH OUR TROUBLES

There are three ways of dealing with our troubles, pains, and adversities.

First, worry about them. Become despondent and despair. Give up and die, for worry does not cure; it kills. It is slow suicide. The world needs your cheer, your personality, your character far more than you are needed in heaven. Remember, the living God will not take his faithful servants out of this world until their tasks have been finished.

The second way to deal with pain and trouble is to do the utmost to get rid of them. Throw them off. Master them. It is not easy; nevertheless, try, try and try again. But, if the trouble will not disappear, what shall we do?

The third thing to do is to resign to its presence. Accept the trouble as sent for some purifying purpose. Then, set about to make it a pearl.

This is what the Apostle Paul did. He called on God for help. God answered. Fortified by God's promise, he received new power. Christ touched him and answered his prayer with the words, "My grace is sufficient for thee."

Exaltingly Paul exclaimed: "I glory in infirmity that Christ may be formed in me." He makes a pearl of his adversity (Read 2 Corinthians 12).

Whom Christ touches He transforms. He touches the blind eyes and they see. He pardons the Magdalene and empowers her for service. And He is able to reinforce our wills and help us to victory. Our troubles may be physical or spiritual. Christ is equal to the difficulty.

It matters not what your life may have been of trouble,

sin, adversity, failure or remorse, Christ the divine al-
chemist can take you and remake you after his likeness. He
can remold broken vessels. He can rebuild your life. He
can tune the discordant soul and heal the broken heart.
With Him you can turn your troubles into blessings.

> The healing of His seamless dress
> Is by our beds of pain
> We touch Him in Life's throng and press
> And we are whole again.

To change the simile, Christ made this harp of a thousand strings which is the human heart. He touches us and
when our wills are submitted to Him He puts life in tune,
however painful the process. Trials are but the testing of
our heart strings, to get them in tune with the heavenly
harmonies whose instruments are all keyed to the note of
eternal love.

Blind George Matheson was touched by the hand of
Christ and his soul glowed with music. His faith was increased, his fears were removed and he cries with a full
heart:

> O Love that will not let me go
> I rest my weary soul in Thee
> I give thee back the life I owe
> That in Thine ocean depths its flow
> May richer, fuller be
>
> O Joy that seekest me thru pain
> I cannot close my heart to thee

I trace the rainbow thru the rain
And feel the promise is not vain
That morn shall tearless be.

We naturally shrink from the testing. But when we look beyond the pain we shall discern the beneficent results: "For I reckon that the sufferings of this present time are not worthy to be compared with the glory that shall be revealed in us" (*Romans 8:18*).

10

What Is Right
with America

Great countries have to deserve to live; they have
to will to live; they have to struggle to live.

—*Lynn Landrum*

SOME OF OUR newspapers and newscasters give the impression that America is one of the worst and most inhuman nations in the world. There is need for revamping our thinking from this negative position.

There are plenty of un-American, un-Christian, unrighteous activities going on in America which anyone can criticize. But all too often we make unfair comparisons between things as they ought to be, and things as they are. We are inclined to become pessimistic. Thus we do not evaluate our beloved America correctly; we paint a lurid picture of evil on the world's historical canvas.

"As a man thinketh in his heart so is he," said the wise man, and it is still true. Christ said it is that which comes out of the heart that defiles the man; such as evil designs, murder, adultery, sexual vice, stealing, false witness, and slander. When men dwell on these ungodly things in their thoughts, they will sooner or later express them in their deeds.

The duty of the Christian is to fill his mind with the best things available in literature, art, pleasure, business, and life as a whole; then he will be able to see things in their right relationships.

Jesus said, "The pure in heart shall see God." It would have been just as true if Jesus had simply said, "The pure in heart shall see." The pure in heart are bound to see the good, the pure, the lovely, the attractive, the honest, the just things in life.

Surely, we must face out facts. We must try honestly to cure the ills in our body politic. But let us be fair in our criticisms, especially about the America we love and honor. We have over 180 millions of people in the United States. Only a small portion of that immense population smears the American canvas of life with crime and injustice. But that tiny minority, in our cities and towns, gets far more publicity and notice than the millions who are the backbone of all our good achievements. Our American men, women, and youths are for the most part able to stand unashamed in integrity, honesty, frugality and in dedication to God, country and the service of mankind, when compared with any people the world over.

Every weakness displayed by an American can be duplicated in the same if not larger proportion in other lands. This message, however, is not intended to be one of odious comparisons with what is wrong, but an exposition of some things that are right.

CHRIST'S INFLUENCE IN AMERICA

Historians, for the most part, have given little emphasis to the effect that Christ has had on the life and influence of America. Christ has changed the life of America for the better, and without His presence America can never be understood. This is a fact, regardless of what historians say or refuse to say. A blind man could say that the sun does not exist, but to say so does not alter the fact that the sun is still in the heavens. One could say that there is no such place as Australia, but that does not disprove the fact that Australia is the largest island continent in the world.

Historians have often overemphasized the divisions within the churches, and discussed the political power sought by the Roman Catholic Church and many non-Catholic churches; but they tend to ignore the dynamic fact that "the living Christ" has been working, and is working, through dedicated men, women, and youths who desire something of the Kingdom of God to be realized within these American shores.

We Americans who have participated in this regeneration have been and are working joyously and enthusiastically under the impelling, persuasive power of Christian love and idealism. This is in absolute contrast to the atheistic Communist who slaves under the coercive, compelling, confiscatory, conscriptive force of the Soviet Socialist states. Christian influence is persuasive, patient, brotherly. The U.S.S.R. is dictatorial, oppressive, tyrannical. Americans, from the Pilgrims of the *Mayflower* to the present, have tried to serve the world under the inner compulsion of the influence of Jesus Christ.

Our American educational development is the outcome of the influence of Christ. The first college, Harvard, was founded under the inspiration of Christ through men who desired the best training for the future Christian ministry and statesmanship of the new nation. Harvard was definitely religious in purpose and program in its early days. The first nine colleges—Harvard, William and Mary, Yale, Princeton, Pennsylvania, Columbia, Brown, Dartmouth, and Rutgers—were established for a Christian purpose. Most of these institutions have Christian declarations within their charters, constitutions, or founding papers.

The University of Pennsylvania was the only college that was not founded by a minister before the eighteenth century; that University was founded by Benjamin Franklin. But he declared the Bible should be a textbook, and he, at one time, said:

> When human science has done its utmost and when we have thought the young worthy of honor, yet still we must recommend them to the Scriptures in order to complete their wisdom, regulate their conduct through life, and guide them to happiness forever.

An American education has its basis in Christ. It is education "under God," and that is right in America.

THE AMERICAN CONSCIENCE

These early Christian educational institutions did much to cultivate what we call the American conscience, which is based on the Christian ethic and can be traced through our social, religious, and governmental development. Whether the critic thinks so or not, it is a fact that America's generosity in national and international disasters is the result of the spirit of Christ that does animate the American conscience. America's generosities are the result of the life and dynamic spirit of the Christ of the American way.

There are, of course, other free nations, but we do not know of any that offers so generous an education to all of her citizens as does the United States. We Americans desire that every boy and girl shall have equal opportunities for intellectual training, and the churches of this great land encourage every boy and girl to accept the opportunity of religious education.

A NATION OF GOOD WILL

America is also right in her motives of service. Enemies and critics of the United States call this country materialistic— more materialistic than any other nation in the world. We can challenge that statement. Perhaps these enemies and critics might have some right to complain, if they were not guilty of crass materialism themselves. Usually people judge others by their own weaknesses. It was the Apostle Paul who asked, "Who art thou that judgeth another? Thou art inexcusable, O man. For wherein thou judgest another thou condemnest thyself, for thou that judgest doest the same things thyself."

We have traveled in many lands where Americans have been bitterly criticized by the very people who have been beneficiaries of America's generosities. If we were to judge these countries only by the few who were discourteous and who said the meanest things about us, we could be more critical of them than they are of us.

When Japan was devastated by floods and earthquakes, America poured into that country food, clothing, and medical aid. If Japan had been inspired through her long history by the "spirit of Jesus Christ," she could never have treacherously attacked us with bombs, submarines, battleships, and instruments of destruction at Pearl Harbor.

If Communist China had been inspired by the same Christ-spirit, she would not have invaded Korea, nor treated her American war prisoners with brainwashing cruelty, as she did with General Dean and other prisoners of war. Neither would she ignore the pledges made in the Korean armistice.

Nor would Communist Russia refuse to "come through clean" if Russian leaders were animated by the Christ-spirit. With that spirit, how different would be the situation throughout the world! The Iron Curtain, the Bamboo Curtain and all the curtains would be lifted and the sunlight of the spirit of freedom and good will would flood the world. Cold and hot wars would cease.

America has kept alive her ideals of human dignity, Christian philanthropy and world service in peace and in war, in her individual and civic and national and international relationships. The influence of Christ in American life has lifted America above the vengeful law of tooth and claw. America is essentially right in her Christian world service program.

MORE THINGS RIGHT THAN WRONG

I love America because she is right in more things than she is wrong. I have dedicated my life and influence to helping my adopted country to turn from all her wicked ways and serve God, giving Him a chance to help America become, more than ever, a bit of the Kingdom of God on earth.

Therefore, it seems to me that Christian Americans ought to rededicate their lives and influence, means and witness, to help bring Russia, China, and all other inimical nations, under the sway of Jesus Christ. We ought not to refuse to go the second mile in Christian service to help all nations learn to dwell together in good will, friendliness and harmony.

America is right in trying to win the enemies of democracy to the liberties we enjoy under Christ. Businessmen are giving more freely of their means. Big business is granting scholarships and economic aid to needy people all over the world. This is the result of the influence of Christ upon them, whether we discern it or not. America is right in continuing to help, regardless of criticism, even by those who are recipients of her generosities. Our international assistance has built irrigation facilities throughout Afghanistan, hospitals in Bolivia, has contributed money and machines to Pakistan to help meet her agricultural needs. Through American assistance, Burma has been rehabilitated. And so on down the long list.

The Kingdom of God will not fully come to America nor to the world until its Spirit takes hold of every individual. There can be no Utopia in America or in the world until there is Utopia in the human heart.

II

Jesus Christ or Karl Marx

> Then said Jesus unto the Twelve, Will ye also
> go away? . . . Then Simon Peter answered Him,
> Lord, to whom shall we go? Thou hast the words
> of eternal life.
>
> —*John 6 : 67, 68*

THIS IS A MODERN question, although it was asked
nearly two thousand years ago. Jesus was "received gladly
by the common people" (*Mark 12:37*). Because of His
sympathetic understanding of the people's problems, all
kinds of people followed Him. His amazing works awakened the rulers as well as the so-called common people.
However, with Jesus, there were no "common" people.
They were *all* prospective, potential children of God.

He was disturbed with the political and religious slavery
of His day. He came to give liberty to the captive, recovery of sight to the blind, to heal the bruised, and to pro-
claim the year of Jubilee, which meant true emancipation.

And multitudes followed Him. The anger of the religious and political rulers was raised by His gospel of freedom (John 12:19).

Thus, when Jesus gave his great discourse about the bread of life, declaring, "I am the bread of life," and that through Him we all may have life here and hereafter, people said, "This is a hard saying" (John 6:60). To them it was a difficult and a strange doctrine, an offensive and an unbearable message. Jesus knew it was difficult for them to accept. He was speaking in terms of the highest freedom when He said that the Spirit gives life, and "the words I speak to you, they are the spirit and they are life."

After that, many of his disciples drew back and went away. Jesus even saw one of His own twelve disciples turning away and, seeing Judas going, He asked, "Will you also go away? Do you desire to leave me?" It was then that Peter answered, "Lord, to whom shall we go? You have the words (the message) of eternal life." Today we are facing an almost identical situation. Because many professing followers of Jesus cannot stand the exclusive, exacting demands of Jesus Christ, they have turned away from Him and go after Karl Marx.

CONTESTING PERSONALITIES

Our Lord Jesus Christ and Karl Marx are the two outstanding contesting personalities in the world scene. Why should these two be brought together in this manner?

In the first place, both Jesus and Karl Marx, by their physical ancestry, were Jews. We are familiar with the birth of Jesus if we have read the Gospels in the New Testament. As for Karl Marx, he was born in Treves in 1818, educated at Bonn, Germany, and participated in revolutionary movements in France. He was exiled to London, where he spent most of his later days in the British Museum studying. Out of these studies came his revolutionary economics. His chief work was *Das Kapital*, which has become the bible of atheistic Communists. He declared that "religion is the opium of the people." Marx died in 1883. But his political and economic immorality lives on, and is one great force which Christianity must deal with and master today.

There is no likeness between our Lord Jesus Christ and Karl Marx as to birth, upbringing, education, and certainly nothing in Marx's career matches Christ's sacrificial, benevolent life or redeeming death. There is little in the teaching of Christ that has any likeness to Marxism, Leninism, Stalinism, or Khrushchevism. Some men, however, appear to think they find some likeness in Christ's emphasis on sharing with that of Karl Marx. Some time ago a young Communist propagandist in Moscow declared that "the teachings of Jesus and Karl Marx are *almost* alike."

It is true that Jesus rebelled against some of the political and immoral standards of His day, and even against some of the religious standards. He met the Sadducees and the Pharisees head on. We recognize Christ's emphasis on the Christian's duty to share with the unfortunate. Jesus did teach his followers to help the poor. Also, Karl Marx demanded that men should share. In this the young Communist propagandist was partly right. But where he was most right was in the use of the word "almost." That word condemns atheistic Communism.

Karl Marx said men must share; that is, men must be

compelled to share. Thus, out of this theory the atheistic Communists demand and practice that men must share by compulsion, by tyrannical force of the totalitarian socialistic state.

THERE IS A DIFFERENCE

Here is the basic difference with any and all of the teachings of our Lord Jesus Christ. The Russian Communists achieve this so-called sharing by using political force, backed by the army, the police force and the nation's whole militant power. Read W. Henry Chamberlain's *Russia's Iron Age* and you will understand. Chamberlain declares that the Communists murdered thousands of little farmers called *kulaks*—the Communists used the word "liquidate" —and sent thousands into exile in Siberian slave camps or to face the firing squad. It is the fearful story of political tyranny by the demoniac, compelling force of organized terror.

Marx says, "Men *must* share"—being first subjugated to force, violence, or any evil method necessary to conquer the world. And the poor, suffering Russians could not and did not understand this. A correspondent for the *Manchester Guardian* wired his paper during the purges: "I have heard the cry of Russia's heart tonight, as I have seen soldiers shoot down a Russian peasant's oldest son." In effect the Russian people were asking their government, "What do you want? We do not understand." That is it. "We do not understand." The loss of the eldest son in Russia is a tragic one. Russian families hope and expect their eldest son to carry on all their traditions. Yet thousands of these fine Russian sons were slain through the *compelling* force of the atheistic soviet-socialist state.

Jesus does ask men to share. But His method is entirely different. It is not even "almost" like Karl Marx.

The law of geometry declares that two straight lines beginning at the same point but not quite parallel become farther apart the farther the lines are extended. That law illustrates the difference between Karl Marx and Jesus. Compare Jesus' method and goal with those of Karl Marx, and the farther you go the farther apart they become. Jesus does require men to share. His great parable of the Good Samaritan is one of His grand examples of Christian sharing. Christ requires men to share, not by tyrannical force but by the ethical and sacrificial power of love. By way of illustrating this dynamic truth, imagine Jesus and Karl Marx beginning to share at the same point. As they move along in their conquest of the world, we find Marx's line is red with the blood of men and women. The line of sharing by Jesus is beautiful with the power of love and Christian brotherhood.

Under Communism there are no Community Chests, no voluntary hospital drives, no deductions on income tax allowable for gifts to schools, colleges, churches, hospitals, orphan homes. By taxation nearly all is taken from the people.

IN COMPARISON

But compare Jesus. You see our Lord standing with open arms saying, "Come unto me, all ye who labor and are overburdened, and I will give you rest. I will ease and relieve and refresh your souls." Hear Christ in his majestic loveliness saying, "If a man compel you to go one mile, go with him, voluntarily, two miles. And if someone comes to you and tries to force you to give him money, do not turn away from him who would borrow (at interest). Help him, if you have it to help him." Again Jesus says, "You have heard how it was said of old-time, You should love your neighbors but hate your enemy, but I say unto you, love your enemies and pray for those who persecute you."

There you have Jesus' pattern of love and brotherly kindness. He not only said, "Share your blessing with others because you love men," but He Himself shared His whole life with all mankind, thus practicing that preaching Himself.

Further, take a look at Calvary. There you see Jesus sharing His life with and for His enemies, as well as for you and me who are His friends. Calvary is the demonstration of God's love. There God was sharing His best with us for the salvation of the world. Christ came to set men free from the bondage of sin, selfishness, hate, lies, vice, and tyranny. God in Christ demonstrates in Himself all He has ever preached in words. He banked all of the success of His redemption on the dynamic force of love.

The whole Russian atheistic Communist experiment, on the other hand, is a sin against the free spirit of men and women. Their whole policy is in conflict with the highest nature of man and of the whole human race. They are determined to control the whole world by force of the military, by their police power, by the employment of lies, de-

ception, untruth, disloyalty, suspicion, and by the enslavement of men's minds and bodies.

Our forefathers did not think that life was so sweet or
peace so cheap that these could be bought for any price.

President Calvin Coolidge, in his reply to Moscow's re-
quest for recognition, during his administration, said: "I
do not propose to barter away for the privilege of trade
any of the cherished rights of humanity. I do not propose
to make merchandise of any American principles. These
rights and principles must go wherever the sanctions of our
government go."

There we have something of the master spirit of Jesus. It
is totally foreign to that of the Marxian Communists.

In a world of confusion and governmental deceptions;
in a world where we boast about the United Nations, we
have a right to ask a question similar to that asked by Jesus:
"Will you also go away into the atheistic Communist fold?"
We answer, with Peter: "Lord, to whom shall we go?
Thou hast the word of eternal life, and we believe and are
sure that Thou art the Christ, the Son of the living God."

12

America—"Great Heart" Among Nations

> I hope we shall never forget that we created this
> nation, not to serve ourselves, but to serve mankind.
> —*Woodrow Wilson*

JOHN BUNYAN, in his *Pilgrim's Progress*, has a character whom he calls "Great Heart" because of his helpfulness to all the needy who cross his path. It is in this sense that we think of America as the "Great Heart" among the nations of the world. Recently, America has come into an atmosphere of unfriendly criticism, even by some of her so-called friends, and by some of the people for whom she has poured out life and means to help in their difficulties.

It is, however, always encouraging to find some upstanding and outstanding citizens of the kingdom of God who speak the facts about this great-hearted land.

Sir Winston Churchill spoke his convictions, saying, in reference to America, "there is no other case of a nation arriving at the summit of world power, seeking no territorial gain, but earnestly resolved to use her strength and wealth in the cause of progress and freedom." And, again, reviewing the sweep of history, and the part other nations played in its movements, he declared, of America that "no other country in all history had shown such generosity toward others."

NOTHING COMPARABLE

There is nothing comparable in world history to the liberality of the American people in world service. In spite of the terrific world tensions, created largely by the untrustworthiness of atheistic Communism, (in Russia and China especially), and in spite of the unparalleled taxation of all classes in our country to pay for foreign aid,—nevertheless, we have been sacrificially generous in our giving of men, money and food in ministry to the sick, in relief to the distressed, in help to the oppressed.

Instead of hoarding our immense resources and products for our own selfish use, America has given away nearly one hundred billions of dollars worth of her products and money since the end of the last world war to help, not only her allies, but also her past or present enemies; this includes Germany, Japan, and even Russia.

Our enemies, and sometimes our careless friends, have spoken profusely about "what's wrong with America". It is always easier and more spectacular to talk about what is wrong than what is right. America has made mistakes, certainly, in an attempt to keep the nations of the world in friendly, cooperative relations. In international as in personal affairs, some friction is bound to occur between the most genial allies and friends. We can, however, be thankful for what God-fearing America has attained in an era of persistent, deliberate, evil misrepresentation by the atheistic Communists. The Kremlin works overtime to discredit every altruistic motive and effort of the United States. Fortunately, they are finding it more and more difficult to make inroads into the great democracies.

God, in His mercy and providence, still is in the American soul. He is watching over us as He did over the founders of this Republic, when He guided them in building the constitution of the American Republic.

Our chief concern today is the same as that of Abraham Lincoln when someone said to him, in the hour of crisis: "I hope that God is on our side" and Mr. Lincoln observed: "My concern is not so much whether God is on our side. My great concern is to be on God's side, because God is always right."

DIVINE IDEALS

American character and liberality is what it is today because our forebears on the rocky New England shores and in sunny Virginia, were from the beginning people of an abiding and dynamic faith in God and in personal freedom.

The warmth of the divine ideals, the passion of a God-given faith, the unconquerable spirit generated by that faith, have led Americans in their sincere endeavor to bring the nations of the world into a world Christian brotherhood and an abiding peace.

No honest thinker could write the history of the United States without giving a large place to the influence of the faithful mothers of our God-fearing leaders and statesmen,

men who represent all phases of American industry, commerce, labor, education, religion and world service. No matter what criticism may be leveled at this land, nevertheless even the most cynical critic must in honesty admit that what is good and true, beautiful, serviceable and beneficial to human welfare, has its roots in the faith of a great people. America's primary faith in God has generated her passion for truth, justice, liberty and the pursuit of happiness for all mankind.

Whenever the moral and spiritual temperature of America has fallen, it has been the resurgence of a dynamic faith in our benevolent and universal God and a firm belief in the ultimate triumph of truth and right, that has inspired, directed, and guided this country back to her divinely appointed destiny.

No matter what the Communistic or jeering cynic may say about American materialism, no thinking person can truly say that when millions of Americans stand before their honored dead on Memorial Day, or on Independence Day, or in their places of worship on Thanksgiving Day, that they are not sincere. Deep in his heart every American knows that there is this principle: "Greater love hath no man than this that a man lay down his life for his friends." Patience and sacrifice is shown even toward our enemies.

BARREN ATHEISM

Atheistic Communists, while tampering with God's moral laws, demonstrate in a farcical and tragic manner how impossible it is to divorce morality from religion, and religion and morality from life, truth, brotherhood and peace. The Communists have tried and are still trying to separate religion from every practical area of life, so that they have had to invent a spurious morality, which they call "The Communistic Dialectic." That means they kick out the great Christian virtues of honesty, integrity and fidelity from the peace conference room. They throw truth and trustworthiness out of the United Nations windows. Liberty, justice, and honor they flush down their Kremlin drain. The Communist's ideological temple is built on the sands of decadent history.

If the pessimistic critic of present-day America will look with open eyes at the full flower of paganism, he will be convinced that America, at her poorest and weakest, is better than paganism at its greatest strength. "By their fruits ye shall know them."

If peddlers of pessimism will study the history of Greece, which is often declared to have been the highest civilization of the ancient world, they will find plenty to shock them. Take the Greek attitude toward children alone, compared with the attitude of the United States. The Greeks gave the father the power to decide whether his child should live or die, or whether he would sell his girl-child into slavery or prostitution. Greek worship was marked with immoral extravagances and even obscenity. One historian has declared that "the Greeks not only saw no value in truth, but practiced perjury as an art, and taught their children to lie." Mercy, as it is understood and practiced by Americans and other Christian peoples, was unknown by the Greeks before the time of Jesus Christ.

FAITH HAS ITS BLESSINGS

Before the Apostle Paul came on the scene of history the words "purity," "love," "friendship," "kindness," "holiness," were unfamiliar terms in the sense that he proclaimed them, or in the sense that we and our children know and practice them. Paul had to invent terms to express these spiritual truths to the Greeks. When we get discouraged we should study how Biblical truth has impregnated our history and how faith in God has made America the Great Heart of the world.

This fact has saturated the literary, political, governmental and educational life of America. It is demonstrated in some of the greatest American government documents and in the addresses and declarations of American statesmen throughout our history. Seldom do any of our presidents speak without expressing some dynamic truth from the Bible. From the declaration of faith by the Pilgrim Fathers in the *Mayflower*, down to President Johnson, our statesmen have emphasized the Christian virtues of faith in God, kindliness, brotherliness, honesty, truth, self-sacrifice, courtesy, liberty, integrity, generosity, service, and have exhorted their fellow Americans to demonstrate these virtues in all their dealings with their fellowmen. Our faith in God expressed by philanthropy and benevolence shows that American history is baptized in the spirit and teachings of Jesus Christ.

Our hearts are saddened when some of our American people refuse to recognize the high moral principles and ideals of our forebears. We are sickened by the overemphasis of human weaknesses in the headlines and pictures of our daily papers and magazines. But we also remember that there are millions of loyal, dedicated Americans who practice the splendor of decency. Thousands of men and women daily demonstrate the integrity of honor, the majesty of manhood, the chivalry that belongs to their strength, the courage of the American character, and the generosity of the American heart.

Some among us, especially those who are naturalized citizens, think of Abraham Lincoln as the symbol of the Great Heart of America. In his farewell address to his neighbors, he said:

> I go to assume a task more difficult than that which devolved upon George Washington. Unless the great God who inspired him shall be with me and inspire me, I must fail. But, if the same omniscient mind and almighty arm that directed and protected him shall guide and support me, I shall not fail. I shall succeed. Let us pray that the God of our fathers will not forsake us now. To Him I commend you all. Permit me to ask that with equal sincerity and faith you will invoke His wisdom and guidance for me—the great God who can stay here with you and go there with me and be everywhere for good.

Lincoln was America at her best.

Through all of Abraham Lincoln's life he symbolized The Great Heart of his beloved country. Why cannot we all do the same and cultivate the same open, forgiving, generous heart in ourselves that we may keep "America the Great Heart of the World."

13

The American
Way of Life

All service ranks the same with God. There is no
last or first.

—*Robert Browning*

IN THE YEAR 1776, on July 4, the American Fathers expressed their hopes and their purposes in the Declaration of
Independence. This is the finest and most succinct statement
of national purpose ever made: "We hold these truths to be
self-evident, that all men are created equal, that they are endowed by their Creator with certain unalienable Rights, that
among these are Life, Liberty, and the pursuit of happiness."

NOT THE MERE DRUDGERY OF LIVING

Notice that the first unalienable right was life. This life is
vastly more than mere existence. It is the abundant life
spoken of by the Master, who "paid his last full measure of
devotion" to give it to everyone who fully and truly
trusted in God.

This trust in God opened up for the Founding Fathers a new experience. They had already found something of the abundant life which the Man of Galilee came to give, and made available to every man, woman and child, regardless of their condition of existence or servitude. Just so, the Founding Fathers wanted to make an abundant life available and possible for all.

There are millions in our world who know nothing about this life which our forefathers had in view. In India, Africa, China, Russia, Cuba, as elsewhere there are multitudes who barely exist on less than the crumbs that fall from their tyrant's, dictator's, or overlord's tables.

The story of the struggles of our early pioneers, braving the stormy Atlantic in frail barques like the *Mayflower*, then enduring the terrific New England winters, and later, the trials of the overland wagon trains, all tell us something of their determination to find "life, liberty and the pursuit of happiness." It was life "in abundance" that these early Americans desired, and for which they struggled, and in a genuine measure achieved.

In establishing the United States they wanted their posterity to enjoy life to the full. This meant some cost to them, requiring a high degree of struggle, dedication and endurance.

All down the American historical pathway we have seen others arriving on our shores, seeking the free life. This is right in the American way. As our Master has put it, "I am come that you might have life and that ye might have it more abundantly."

PURSUIT OF HAPPINESS IN LIBERTY

In the achievement of this life, there was also to be full and abundant liberty to enjoy the "pursuit of happiness." This abundant liberty, of necessity, had to be limited by the citizen's willingness to accept responsibilities and obligations. This full and overflowing liberty was also something new under the sun. No other nation had known anything of this ideal which gave birth to the United States of America. In the lands whence the Founding Fathers came, there were only a few liberties for them. Thus, in the new land, they wanted an overflowing liberty, limited only by the moral circumference of Christian brotherhood.

I refer to Christian brotherhood because this is where true liberty is found. Physical brotherhood is not enough. We all know of instances where some of the meanest and worst divisions, even tragedies, have occurred within families where brothers disagreed. Even in so-called fraternal brotherhoods labor, industrial, even national brotherhoods, many disappointments have occurred. Brothers have murdered brothers, as Cain killed Abel, his brother in the flesh. Kaiser Wilhelm made war against the King of England, his close relative, in 1914. But in the realm of true Christian brotherhood, there is a new element, *viz.*, friendship. The Bible speaks of that new element which does guarantee sensible, sane, patient persistence in solving problems within the Christian brotherhood. The Bible says, "If a man would have friends he must show himself friendly, and there is a friend who sticks closer than a brother." In his brotherhood all race problems find solution.

Liberty is another of the unalienable rights in the American way of life and happiness. Americans must learn, as should all peoples, that liberty is never limited. Liberty, as stated in the Declaration of Independence, means there is no limitation of liberty to do good, to be decent, and to achieve the highest service for God and country in our "pursuit of happiness."

Those who have unusually large talents must use and improve them intellectually, physically, financially and spiritually, for the uplift of the lesser talented citizens, who sincerely strive to make the best of what they have. Just so, those of us who may seem to have just one talent must strive to use that one talent to the fullest extent of our abilities, and determine to rise intellectually, economically and culturally in our pursuit of happiness for ourselves and for our fellow citizens.

The American way is right in its pursuit of life and liberty for all citizens and for all men everywhere on earth.

THE PRICE OF HAPPINESS

Why do we need freedom for our pursuit of happiness? After all, only happy people are the truly successful people. The happy people are the easiest people with whom to work and have fellowship. Unhappy people make it difficult for the happy people to work with them and serve them. This is another reason why the Founding Fathers emphasized the unalienable right to *pursue* happiness. That word "pursue" is a good one. It means that every American must ever be alerted to the needs of his fellows, especially to those less fortunate who may be in their present difficulty through no fault of their own.

This is where our Founding Fathers were right. They

wanted every man to have equal opportunity to improve himself to the utmost of his capabilities. This means strenuous living. Many Americans, unfortunately, are unwilling to burn the midnight oil to improve themselves. But others, who are successful, have toiled long into the night while their fellow students have slept their opportunities away.

Now, today, many, both white and black, are demanding so-called equal rights, but are unwilling to pay the price of climbing the ladder step by step. They now want to get to the top quickly, without mental or physical exertion. Success really depends on what we each possess within. Everyone must build something of an inner spiritual power within himself. We must possess knowledge, will power, energy and persistence. What is inside us makes us or breaks us.

George Washington Carver was not a great scientist because he was born a Negro slave. He got out of slavery, and by dedication rose above poverty and mediocrity. He used what he possessed. He took every opportunity to better himself and his character and to master the mean things which tried to hold him down; the same things which have kept multitudes of unhappy Negro and white people in mental, moral and spiritual slavery. The pursuit of happiness, in America, is limited only by one's inner space of mental, moral and spiritual dynamics. The most underprivileged man can win if he thinks he can and will pay the price of self-mastery, self-sacrifice, self-control, and develop a living trust in God and in himself, just as did the scientist, George Washington Carver, and multitudes of other Americans, black, white, red and yellow. All things are possible to him who trusts in God and does his best.

THE OPPORTUNITY IS HERE

I would remind my fellow Americans that there are still opportunities for white and colored, and for all minorities within America, to live abundantly and be happy citizens. Many of our American Negroes have achieved this life in material and spiritual ways. There are more Negroes in America who own their own homes than in any other country, including all of Europe and all the Communist countries. American Negroes own more automobiles, hold more college degrees, own more electric appliances for their comforts than all other Negroes in the world. In spite of the inequalities in some areas, the Negro in America is better off in every way than in any other country.

If we all come under the influence of the God in whom we trust and if all will give their best, be their best and do their best, these inequalities will be overcome; just as George Washington Carver, the scientist; Booker T. Washington, the humanitarian; Ralph Bunche, the diplomat; and hundreds of other Negroes and whites have overcome. These men were not afraid of work but concentrated on thought and spiritual growth. Men are not born equal. We all know that, even in our own families. But, thank God! America is right in her way of life, liberty and happiness.

From the beginning, America has believed that every human soul is of the highest worth. We have recognized the vast differences of individual abilities; but we also believe we should make it possible for everyone to have equal opportunities. Our universal education has come into being because of this belief.

CITIZENS OF HOPE

The American way of life is also right because it is the way of hope. From the beginning, when the *Mayflower* anchored in Plymouth Bay, all aboard were "citizens of hope." They hoped for better days; they hoped for life, for freedom, for happiness. They hoped for a country wherein men could stand erect, with the love of God in their hearts and the love of mankind in their eyes, and the love of world service in their souls. They longed for, worked for, and had faith that they could produce a country without the fear of repression. Through joy and sadness, through tragedy and success, each generation has produced many uncommon men and women who have been dedicated to help fulfill America's destiny.

Listen to a great statement from one of the men who helped formulate the American way of life. We need his spirit reborn in every heart today. It would help our politicians, and disgruntled Americans in general, to read and ponder his words as he declared himself in favor of the Declaration of Independence. I quote John Adams, who is reported by Daniel Webster to have said:

Sink or swim, live or die, survive or perish, I give my hand and my heart to this vote. It is true, indeed, that in the beginning, we aimed not at independence, but "there is a divinity that shapes our ends." The injustice of England has driven us to arms: And, blinded to her own interests, she has obstinately persisted, till independence is now within our grasp. . . .

Sir, I know the uncertainty of human affairs, but I see, I see clearly, through this day's business. You and I indeed may rue it. We may not live to see the time when this declaration shall be made good. We may die: die slaves: die, it may be, ignominiously and on the scaffold. Be it so. If it is the pleasure of heaven that my country shall require the poor offering of my life, the victim shall be ready at the appointed hour of sacrifice, come when that hour may; but, while I do live, let me have a country, or at least, the hope of a country and that a free country.

Sir, before God, I believe the hour is come. . . . All I have, and all I am and all that I hope in this life, I am ready here to stake upon it: And I leave as I began that, live or die, survive or perish, I am for this Declaration. It is my living sentiment and by the blessing of God, it shall be my dying sentiment—Independence now and Independence forever.

Independence cannot truthfully be enjoyed without responsibility. This is a real need, if we are in earnest. We are not for freedom if it is used only to practice evil. We believe in good citizenship. The kind that seeks the best for our country and the world, to the glory of its Creator. To that end we will oppose everything that shackles the souls of men and women to practices that are fundamentally wrong. We covet a nation of people dedicated to God and to the freedoms He inspires in the hearts of men.

14

America's Spiritual Heritage

... The way is plain, peaceful, generous, just—
a way which, if followed, the world will forever
applaud and God must forever bless.

—Abraham Lincoln

IMPOSING STATUES of Abraham Lincoln are found
on almost all the continents. Although Mr. Lincoln never
united with a church, he has been claimed by most of the
churches; I think, because of his outstanding Christian
spirit, regardless of any personal weaknesses he might have
had. We are sure that the churches today would all be
stronger and more effective in the whole life of America
and the world, if they were filled with members of the
spirit and character of Abraham Lincoln.

In so many ways he expresses the embodiment of the
true "Uncle Sam." To study the life and deeds of Lincoln is to become convinced that the mantle of the Founding Fathers fell upon his shoulders. Their faith in God and

God's power over these dedicated men seemed transferred to Abraham Lincoln. In many ways Lincoln was almost a miracle man: born in the obscurity of a log cabin, having but a year of traditional school training, he became a truly great thinker, an orator of unusual power, a constructive writer and of course, President of the United States of America. Of him, Walt Whitman said, "I should say the invisible foundations and vertebrae of Lincoln's character, more than any man in history, were moral and spiritual, while upon all of them was built what the vulgar call 'horse sense.'"

THE NEW GENERATION

We are confident that our new generations would be stronger, more vigorous, more Christian, and more patriotic, if they would follow the pathway Lincoln took in his boyhood. Lincoln loved to read and study. He knew how to concentrate and to absorb what he read. His first books were the Bible, Pilgrim's Progress, the lives of Benjamin Franklin and George Washington. He transmitted the best of these books into his own thinking and character. Washington and Franklin knew God through faith and experience. Just so, Lincoln became a personal friend of God, and felt God was his Friend. He believed God was ordering his life.

In his farewell statement before leaving Springfield, he said, "Without the assistance of that Divine Being I cannot succeed. With that assistance I cannot fail. Trusting Him who can go with me and remain with you, and be everywhere for good, let me confidentially hope that all will be well. To His care commending you as I hope in your prayers you will commend me, I bid you an affectionate farewell." Lincoln did trust in God.

Lincoln expressed his trust in God throughout his public life. In Buffalo, he said, "I must trust in that Supreme Being who has never forsaken this favored land." In Columbus, he declared, "I turn to God for support who has never forsaken the people." In Steubenville, he exclaimed, "Nothing shall be wanting on my part if sustained by the American people and God." In Albany, he spoke, "I still have confidence that the Almighty Maker of the universe will bring us through this." In Trenton, he expressed his trust, "I shall be most happy indeed if I shall be an humble instrument in the hands of the Almighty and of the most chosen people, as a chosen instrument, also in the hands of the Almighty, of perpetuating the object of this great struggle."

COURAGE AND HONESTY

In that spirit Lincoln lived. His courage and his honesty came from this overwhelming conviction that Almighty God had a work for him to do, and he meant to be faithful to that conviction. He backed that up by saying, "I have nothing said but that I am willing to live by, and if it be the pleasure of Almighty God, to die by." And he did.

Lincoln also believed in another great Christian doctrine, the perseverance of the saints. The doctrine of perseverance became a part of his life from the beginning to the end. He believed that "he that endureth to the end shall be saved." His mother said to him just before she died, "I am going away from you Abraham, and shall not return. I know that you will be a good boy and that you will be kind to your father. I want you to live as I have taught you, to love your Heavenly Father and keep His commandments." Lincoln kept faith with his mother and God.

His biographies all show he had temptations a-plenty in his legal career. He stood unmovable. Someone wrote, "He was the most honest man west of China."

Lincoln's mother left a deposit of honesty, fidelity, devotion, and spiritual gold so that her son was able to say, "All that I am and all I hope to be I owe to my angel mother." Perseverance in faith and good was fundamental in Lincoln's life.

Lincoln had no creed but the Bible. He was saturated with the Bible. His speeches are filled with quotations and allusions to the Scriptures. One day he used it in a humorous manner, during a debate with Douglas. When Douglas laughed at Lincoln's long, gaunt stature, and cried out, "How long, oh Lord, how long!" Lincoln, not at all taken aback, also quoted Scripture to describe his short, stubby opponent: "Remember, the Book says, 'The wicked shall be cut off.' "

Lincoln's closing declaration in his Gettysburg address, "Government of the people, by the people, for the people," was a quotation from the preface of Wycliffe's Bible. And his quotation in his great address, "A house divided against itself cannot stand, neither can a country half slave and half free," was also inspired by God's word.

Lincoln believed in the separation of church and state. He declared, "The United States government must not undertake to run the churches. Let the churches take care of themselves." We now have the pressure of a great hierarchy to get their hands on the United States Treasury for the support of their sectarian and parochial schools. We do need men who stand unequivocably for what Lincoln declared.

FREEDOM FOR ALL

Religious liberty was another cardinal belief of Lincoln's. When a movement started to prohibit Roman Catholic ritual and ceremonies, Lincoln introduced a resolution in an Illinois convention declaring that religious liberty—the right of conscience—belongs as truly to the Roman Catholic as it does to the Protestant.

Lincoln was dedicatedly opposed to force or violence in religion and in government. That was a matter between the individual and his God. Lincoln would be today the most outspoken antagonist against religious tyranny just as he would be against Communist and any other tyranny. Where did Lincoln get these ideas? From his mother's knee to his death, God was sovereign to him.

His father and mother were members of the Pidgen Creek Baptist Church, in what was then Warren County, Indiana territory. Lincoln's father and Nancy Hanks were married by a Methodist minister, but they both later united with a Baptist church in the Licking-Locust Association of regular Baptist churches in Kentucky. Abraham Lincoln's mother, Nancy Hanks Lincoln, was buried in Indiana near a Baptist Church in 1828, and Lincoln personally arranged for Elder Elkins to come from the Kentucky church to give a funeral message over the grave. Almost everything that happened to Lincoln seemed to him to be the providence of God.

Abraham Lincoln took God as his anchor in storm. It is recorded he heard that a group of ministers, twenty-three of them, had planned to vote against him as a presidential candidate. They cut him to the heart, because they thought him to be a free thinker, an unbeliever and, perhaps, an infidel.

He took from his pocket a New Testament with which he was as thoroughly familiar as any of the twenty-three preachers, and his voice vibrated with deep emotion as he said, "These men know well that I am for freedom in the territories, freedom everywhere, free as the Constitution and the laws of the land will permit, and that my opponents are for slavery. They know this, and yet with this Book in their hands, in the light of which human bondage cannot exist for a moment, they are going to vote against me. I do not understand this at all." He paused a moment, his eyes moist and his body shaking with emotion. He spoke as a prophet and said, "I know there is a God, and that He hates slavery. I see a storm coming, and I know that His hand is in it. If He has a place for me, and I believe He has, I believe I am ready. I am nothing. Truth is everything. I know I am right, because I know that liberty is right, for Christ teaches it and Christ is God. I have told them, a house divided against itself cannot stand, and Christ and reason say the same. And they will find it so.

"Douglas does not care whether slavery is voted up or down, but God cares and I care, and with God's help I shall not fail. I may not see the end, but it will come and I shall be vindicated, and these men will find that they have not read their Bibles aright."

That was Lincoln's faith, and what a declaration of Christian faith! History has vindicated him.

What an example of faith and dedication to God and

America, is here displayed. If our politicians would put God and their country first and second and their party and themselves third, God's prophecy for America, as for Israel, will come true and be realized in our day. God says, "Righteousness exalteth a nation." Faith is the victory that overcomes the world of atheistic Communism and corrupt government, corrupt business, corrupt labor, corrupt theatrical performances, and corrupt literature. Faith is the victory that overcomes the world, the whole world of badness everywhere.

A REVERENT COMPARISON

While studying the faith of Lincoln, I made an interesting comparison between Lincoln and Christ. I do this reverently and without any implication that Lincoln was as divine as Christ.

Christ was born in a stable, Lincoln in a log cabin. Joseph was a carpenter, Lincoln's father was a carpenter. Jesus was a lover of stories, Lincoln was a great storyteller. Christ was without form or comeliness, as the prophet Isaiah described Him. This was true of Lincoln. Christ was a man of sorrows and acquainted with grief. And was that not true of Lincoln? Jesus was a Hebrew name and so was Lincoln's, Abraham.

Both met death on what we call "Good Friday." This all seems a part of Lincoln's belief that he was under the hand of God. Lincoln always had a hope of taking Mrs. Lincoln to the Holy Land to see the places where the Lord worked and did His wonderful ministry. It is told that on the evening at the theater, Lincoln was saying to Mrs. Lincoln, "Dear, we do hope we shall soon be able to visit the Holy

Land together, go to Nazareth, Bethlehem, Jericho, Jerusalem." But he did not finish that word Jerusalem, because a shot rang out and Lincoln fell, not to speak again, so that he must have finished that word in the New Jerusalem. And as Stanton said, when the President was dead, "Now he belongs to the ages."

Would it not be wonderful if we Americans could and would elect to positions of leadership, and offices of trust, men who can and will practice and say what Lincoln said, "You may burn my body to ashes and scatter them to the four winds of Heaven. You may drag my soul down to the regions of darkness and despair to be tormented forever, but you will not get me to support a measure that I believe to be wrong."

Thank God, we have some men like that today. We need many more. These are the "salt of the earth." These are the "light of our world." These are the "anchors of our Christian democracy."

Let it be said of all of us, as Lincoln said of himself, "Die when I may, I want it said of me by those who knew best, that I always plucked a thistle and planted a flower where I thought a flower would grow."

15

The Ultimate
Triumph of Right

The life of Christ, therefore, both as revelation and as sacrifice, is taken to be the activity in time of God Himself. All that Jesus was in Himself, and all that He said and did, was predicated of God. As revelation, the Logos; as servant, the Son; as sacrifice, the Lamb of God. The total significance of Jesus may be expressed thus: The Revealer of the divine ideal in the perfect life establishes that ideal through reconciliation accomplished by sacrifice. As Harnack says: "The paradox of Christianity is that the Creator is also the Redeemer."

—Louis Matthews Sweet

MELANCHOLY THINKERS speak of the "downfall of Christianity"; dyspeptic religionists moan and wail about the "collapse of the Christian Church"; despondent theorists raise their plaintive cries concerning "the bankruptcy of religion." A pessimist poet sings of "The Funeral of God."

We acknowledge that the cause of Christ is being put

through the acid test. Nevertheless, we declare with hopeful emphasis that while we do not as yet "see all things put under Him," we do know Jesus Chirst is the world's hope. It is Jesus Christ who gives us every confirmation of our confidence in the ultimate triumph of right in the world.

Before the mountains are scaled many a bog must be crossed, and many a discouraging path must be traveled. Fogs may obscure the mountain tops; nevertheless, beyond the mists and miasmas of the low-lying swampland rises the snow-clad peaks of the Himalayas; storms may burst in terrible fury on the Cascades, but afterwards the clouds will pass away and Mt. Hood, unmoved, stands forth in magnificence and grandeur.

As surely as night precedes day, as certainly as dawn comes after midnight, and as positively as sunshine follows clouds, so will Christianity march from apparent defeat to glorious and inevitable triumph.

> Truth and right may be
> . . . forever on the scaffold,
> Wrong forever on the throne.
> Yet that scaffold sways the future.
> And behind the dim unknown
> Standeth God within the shadow,
> Keeping watch above his own.

Justice, right, and truth are bound to win.

IT HAS BEEN DARK BEFORE

Christianity has faced darker days than this present. Christianity thrives on persecution and struggle. The aggressive cynicism of the atheist, the withering criticism of the materialist, and the subtle aspersions of the skeptic have not disproved the truth nor the power of Christianity. They have rather served Christianity by revealing the emptiness of religious ritualism and emphasizing the disintegrating force of intolerant sectarianism. Formalism is void of spiritual power. It is the modern outward show and the deception of formalism that is bankrupt.

When we cut through the ceremonial garments and hew away the accretions and accumulations that have covered and obscured the heart of Christianity for ages, we discover that a living Person is working in the world with tremendous effectiveness, transforming personalities through His redemptive grace.

The church does face some alarming situations. But these do not spell defeat. They are warnings, and a challenge to the church for a cultured, consecrated, spirit-filled, positive, dynamic ministry and membership. The whole present situation is God's bugle call to crown Christ Lord of all, and to make His cross operative in our lives and deeds.

God is not dead. Jesus Christ is not bankrupt. His resources are not played out. True, thousands will have nothing to do with Him. But because men refuse to do His bidding, it is no evidence of the inefficacy of His ethics or the unworkableness of His rule. One's refusal to take a bath is no evidence that water will not cleanse. To refuse to eat does not prove that food has lost its power to nourish. Is Christ impotent to save because I refuse His offer of pardon? Is He powerless to redeem because I resist Him and deny His authority by my stubborn will?

Too many lives have been voluntarily sacrificed for our Lord Jesus Christ to have Christianity fail. Millions have

> Climbed the steep ascent to heaven
> Through peril, toil and pain;

and millions today are ready to stand persecution and death for Christ and His Gospel's sake.

THERE IS A FUNDAMENTAL RIGHT

Christianity will triumph because it is fundamentally right. "God was in Christ reconciling the world unto Himself." The great task of the church is to rightly present Jesus's view of God to the world. Jesus's teaching concerning the Fatherhood of God is the only true basis of world brotherhood and universal peace.

The love of God expressed by Christ cannot be narrowed down within the limits of any race or national exclusiveness. God's love breaks down barriers set up by the prejudices of men. He reaches out to the ends of the earth in pity and sympathy, to lift up all men out of the whirlpool of sin and to make them "kings and priests unto God." We shall never surpass the practical nor the theological conception of salvation as given by Jesus Christ, who reveals and expresses God as a Father loving and seeking His lost children.

THE GOLDEN RULE IS DYNAMIC

Christianity, being fundamentally right, will triumph because the message of Jesus concerning individual relation-

ships will never be surpassed. His principle of the Golden
Rule will never be outmoded. So far as history is concerned,
there is only one person who has dared to practice the
Golden Rule in all of its ramifications. No one else seems to
have been courageous enough to take this great adventure.
They have failed when it was necessary to "forgive sev-
enty times seven." They have allowed selfish interests to
control when the Golden Rule meant selfless service. To
make the Golden Rule dynamic in life requires more courage than it does to face a battery of guns. But wherever the
Golden Rule has been attempted, it has never failed.

Let the nations apply this Golden Rule to their own
problems, and especially to international affairs; and they
will attempt the most courageous program ever under-
taken by any people.

If the Golden Rule were put to work in the home, the
state, and the nation, we would see the most marvelous
transformation in economics, in our living, and in human
relationships. When employer and employee, rich and poor,
learned and unlearned, politician and businessman, husband
and wife, courageously put the Golden Rule into action, a
new society will be born. Men are inclined to say that to
practice the Golden Rule between nations would be insan-
ity. No, it would be the greatest act of faith and reason
ever attempted. The world is waiting one nation with the
courage to put the Golden Rule into practice in all of its
applications.

Because the Golden Rule strikes at every basic human
relationship, it requires spiritual power to apply it and to
work it in everyday contacts. Jesus supplies the divine dy-

namic of victorious living. With His aid we are "more than conquerors." Wherever Jesus Christ enunciates a principle of living, He is eternally right.

THE SPIRIT OF SERVICE

Right will triumph because Christianity glories in its ministry of redemptive service. Before Jesus Christ came, who thought of service to others? Men came to be ministered unto. They did not come to minister. Jesus came "to minister and give His life as ransom for many." Before His coming kings, rulers, men of power, had no passion to serve their fellow men. Selfishness ruled and controlled them. Jesus Christ has fired His followers with a new passion. Nothing less than world service can satisfy Christ's man or woman. The cross and the "towel and basin" have become symbols of Christ's unselfish abandon to redeem mankind. The dynamic of the cross of Calvary has thrust out thousands of men and women into home and foreign service. His spirit has made Christian philanthropists and fired them with unselfish zeal. The whole missionary program is evidence that Christ lives today.

Jesus Christ is unique. His is a different spirit from the rest of mankind. He wants to make mankind like unto Himself. No one ever surpassed His unselfishness. His utter abandonment to the service of others finds its perfect illustration in His life at every turn. He gave no command that He had not first obeyed. He did not urge anyone to do that which He was not willing to do, or which He Himself had not already done. He sets the ideal and furnishes His conquering spirit to every earnest, sincere, surrendering sinner. Because of His love for mankind He lays the foundations of justice, liberty, brotherhood, purity of life and motive. These are basic to world service.

Christianity has the inherent power of recovery and revival. The dark ages came; so did the Reformation. Pride, arrogance, lethargy, unconcern followed. It looked as if Christianity would die of dry rot. Then burst forth the Wesley revival. So through the years. Christianity has had many setbacks in recent days. Men are asking old questions: "Will the church survive? Will the face of Christ be obliterated? Will the religion of Christ be eradicated and all Christianity liquidated?" Far more skillfully than Karl Marx or any of his followers, Augustine plumbed the depths of the soul when he said: "Thou hast made us for Thine own and our hearts are restless until they find rest in Thee."

Unbelievers have always taunted the church. Ridicule is their favored weapon. There have been darker days than today. When Titus crucified so many that he could not find crosses for more men marked for crucifixion, he doubtless cried: "Where is the supremacy of Jesus Christ today!"

BUT GOD INTERVENED

The triumph of Christ is not spectacular. It comes not with observation. The miracle of Christianity is Christianity itself. To think that twelve humble disciples fired with the conviction that Christ is able to cause the most profound spiritual revolution in the world's most discouraging situation—this is the marvel of the ages. Within the circumference of a few years the world was being saturated with the spirit of the living Christ. And all down the ages the highest intellects of the world have surrendered to His ideals and become slaves to His high morality. The indestructible vitality of Christianity is guaranteed by the stupendous fact of the resurrection of Jesus Christ. It is a constantly reviving cause.

There is in every sincere student of the Bible and of history, a strong conviction that Jesus Christ is all He claims to be. They are sure that if He had half a chance in this world of men and governments, He would bring in that glorious day when the angels' song should be realized: "Peace on earth, and good will to men." No teacher has ever made, or is making, stronger appeals to the hearts and minds of men and to human conscience than is Jesus Christ at this hour.

We cannot get away from Jesus Christ. The indifference, lethargy and unconcern of many may allow the mechanistic legions to crucify Christ afresh. The apathy of the people in general may allow Him to be put into the grave of materialistic theories and philosophic vagaries; but more sure than the sun will arise on tomorrow, will our Lord Christ break the bars of prejudice and roll away the stone of intolerance and come forth more radiantly and more joyously triumphant than on the first Easter Day.

> I cannot put His presence by; I meet Him
>   everywhere;
> I meet Him in the country town and in the
>   market square;
> The mansion and the tenement proclaim His
>   presence there.

Upon the funnelled ships at sea He sets
   His shining feet;
The distant ends of empire not in vain His
   name repeat;
And like the fragrance of a rose He makes
   the whole world sweet.

He comes to break the barriers down set
   up by barren creeds;
Across the world from zone to zone like
   sunlight he proceeds;
He comes to give the world's starved heart
   the perfect love it needs.

The Christ, whose friends oft played Him
   false, whom dogmas have belied,
Still speaking to the hearts of men though
   slain and crucified,
The Master of the Centuries, who cannot be
   denied.

Christianity has had its ebb and flow; but the tide has
been steadily rising. The sun may be obscured by clouds of
worldliness, unfaithfulness, materialism, unbelief; but the
Sun of Righteousness shall rise with healing in His wings.

On Easter Sunday morning, I stood on a beautiful hill in
California, proclaiming the gospel of the resurrection.
When I left home, it was intensely dark. Except for the
light of the stars, men would hardly have found their way
up the hillside to the sunrise service. But just as the large
congregation sang "All Hail the Power of Jesus' Name,"

the sun burst forth in all its beauty and glory, flooding the hills and the far valleys with light and warmth until the whole country basked in its life-giving radiance. So it is to-day. Christianity may be passing through a long antarctic night. Day after day, month after month, passes by. The only light is from a star here and there. But in God's good time He will tilt the world in the direction of fulfilment of Christ's promise; and our Lord will come in all His kingly glory. The night of ignorance, superstition, prejudice, hate, intolerance, violence, will pass away in the brightness of His coming; and the whole world shall dwell in the brilliance of Eternal Day.

16

Imperatives for the Space Age

> No free government or the blessings of liberty can be preserved to any people but by a firm adherence to justice, moderation, temperance, frugality and virtue, and by a frequent recurrence to fundamental principles.
>
> —*Patrick Henry*

THREE AGES have been thrust upon us in our lifetime. (1) The Russian Revolution has pressured us into an age of revolution. (2) The atomic bomb has blasted us into the nuclear age and placed in our hands power ten million times more devastating or more constructive than any previous generation possessed. (3) The space age has been forced upon us by the first satellite fired into 'the blue sky yonder,' which threatens that whole nations could be cremated in a few hours.

The Air Force recently released these alarming facts: Should a nuclear war begin, within 24 hours 53 large cities would be destroyed; 40 per cent of the American people would be dead. The same would be true of the enemy. Of the remaining 60 per cent, millions would suffer leukemia, bone cancer, and other mutilating diseases. There would be nothing to gain for us or the enemy that would be worth the price of an atomic war.

These discoveries have opened up to us undreamed-of dimensions, not only of space but of fear and terror; and, thank God, also of faith and hope. Never before have we faced such possibilities for good or evil. Do we have what it takes?

We may not be able to do much about outer space at present, but what of the inner space world? Scientists say the nation that masters *outer* space will conquer the world. Actually, it is the nation that controls *inner* space that will serve the best.

WE MUST DEAL WITH OURSELVES FIRST

One may ask, "What do you mean by *inner* space?" Exactly what Jesus meant when he asked, "What shall it profit a man if he gain the whole world and lose his soul?" What shall it profit America if it gain the whole world of outer space and lose its soul of inner space?

In this inner-space world have been bred bigotry, fears of war, fears of extinction, fears of hellish suffering. These fears have already aggravated some people into recklessness, and even to suicide. Our politicians do not seem too concerned about conscience in this inner-space world or they would encourage a higher morality in all phases of governmental and civic life.

I refuse to be pessimistic about the alarming space possibilities, because I believe God lives and still holds the whole world of nature's powers and laws in His hands. We cannot discount, however, a disturbing possibility that even now some Communist nation may have a satellite loaded with atomic destruction that could be fired at any moment by some insane, vodka-crazed leader.

Atheistic Communism has already downgraded human beings to the level of animals through its materialistic dialectic. Communists have become past-masters in propagandizing hate, fraud, deception to achieve their ends.

Communists have taken the slogan, "The end justifies the means," and adapted it to their imperialistic ends. These matters all relate to inner space. Lenin, the high priest of Communism, himself said (*Lenin's Selected Works*, Vol. 5, p. 147):

> Hate for one's government—the sentiment of all class-conscious workers . . . is a banal phrase, if it does not mean revolution against their governments. It is impossible to rouse hatred against one's government and one's bourgeoisie without desiring their defeat.

And the *Congressional Record* (Vol. 55, p. 1538) states that Anatole Lunacharsky said:

> We must hate. . . . Hatred is the basis of Communism. Children must hate, be taught to hate their parents if they are not Communists. We hate Christians and Christianity. Even the best of them must be considered our worst enemies. Christian love is an obstacle

to the development of the Revolution. Down with love to one's neighbors. What we want is hate, only hate. Then we will conquer the universe.

Here is the doctrine according to Satan for you. This is pumped into the minds of Russian children and students. A few disillusioned Americans would have this stuff siphoned into the minds of American youth. Let us be warned by the Word of God which states: "As a man thinketh in his heart (his *inner space*), so is he." Also, "Can a man take fire unto his bosom and not be burned?"

SOME IMPERATIVES

This is where the imperatives come in for American citizens and especially Christians. The witnessing of the gospel of reconciliation with conviction, certitude, and divine enthusiasm was imperative with Jesus and His disciples. The gospel deals with the whole area of man's inner space. Right here is the cause of world trouble, the cold war, the confusion of tongues, the explosiveness of social, economic, political, and even religious conditions. Yes, all of these are "inner-space" matters.

The two paramount imperatives for American patriots in this space age are:

First, a divine certitude that "In God We Trust" is more than just words. We must be sure of God, as was Jesus Christ sure of Himself. He was a perfect example of conviction, assurance, and certitude. He was sure of His message, positive of His mission, and supremely certain of His Messiahship. Jesus spoke with a divine affirmation. "You must be born anew." "The Son of Man is come to seek and to save that which was lost." "I must work the works of him that sent me while it is day." "I must be about my Father's business," and so on. Christ's certitude amazed all who heard Him. They exclaimed, "He spoke as one having authority, not as the scribes."

The Apostles followed in His steps. Paul said, "I know whom I have believed and am persuaded that He is able to meet all my needs." John exclaimed, "That which we have heard, which we with our own eyes have seen, which we have looked upon, and with our own hands have handled of the Word of Life, that we declare unto you." There is divine dogmatism. This space age demands that of us today.

The certitude about which I am writing is not the materialistic dogmatism of the Communists. There is nothing of their demonic negativism in the message or attitude of Jesus and His disciples. The Communists promise what they know they cannot deliver, but Christian patriots can produce what Jesus promises when they translate His message of reconciliation into everyday practice in their homes, in the schools, in business and in industry; in our political and social organizations, and in our churches. Christian conviction and certitude are urgently imperative now.

WHO IS TO CONVERT THE MASSES?

The Apostles were so sure of Christ and of His gospel that miracles attended their ministry wherever they went; whereas, today, some ministers and American Christians are so completely unsure, uncertain, about nearly everything, that they cannot raise even a ripple on the dead sea of their lethargy and unconcern. Negative witnessing of doubts and what we do not believe can never convert the masses, nor arouse the indifferent to Christian action. People do not go to church to hear ministers preach doubts— they have too many of their own. People need the Almighty's affirmations, his supreme securities, his Christlike certitudes.

It must have been a "dispenser of doubts" of whom the Scotsman spoke when he said, "We have a strange minister in our kirk. In the week he is invisible and on Sunday he is incomprehensible. He lacks authority and carries no conviction."

There was no uncertainty with the Apostles. They could say with the healed blind man of *John 9*, "I may not know all about the how, or the why, or even the who, but this one thing I know: whereas, I was blind, now I see." There is no equivocation, mental reservation, or secret evasion about that witness. There must be none in ours.

The other urgent imperative is the burning heart and the tongue of fire for the space age. The ministry in America must be sustained by a baptized intellect, a heart aflame, and a tongue of fire from the Holy Spirit. John Calvin's crest was the burning heart and the open hand. If the Christian ministry had always cultivated a God-controlled intellect, kept the burning heart aflame, preached with the tongue of fire the gospel witness for Christ, Mark Twain would never have thus characterized the ministry of his day, "Their minds were never loaded with anything but blank cartridges," nor would ministers be what the Bible calls "prophets of wind." The true symbol of the Apostolic ministry is not vestments or ritual, but the tongue of fire and the heart aflame and the open hand. Enthusiasm is an Apostolic imperative. It is contagious.

The word enthusiasm comes from two Greek words; *en* —meaning in or through or from—and *theos*—meaning God. Thus Paul spoke about "in Christ" and "through Christ." Professor Deisman, the German scholar, says these terms or their equivalents are recorded over 163 times in New Testament epistles. Is it any wonder that the Apostle Paul could say, "I can do all things through Christ who energizes me."

Christian Americans, with hearts aflame, can overcome despondency, discouragement, defeat. Enthusiasm creates and cultivates perseverance. Judson in Burma, Zackery in Zanzibar, Morrison in China, are excellent missionary examples of this—laboring for years without seeing a convert, yet never quitting.

Our world now needs the compulsion of the burning heart, but a large part of it is expressing itself with the clenched fist. Atheistic Communism has profaned the New Testament symbol of the burning heart and replaced it with fanatical zeal and the clenched fist of intolerance, regimentation, and bloody revolution. This is expressed in Khrushchev's theme song: "We will bury you who disagree with us."

MEETING THE THREAT

We have two extremes of the burning heart facing each other today. The modern world negative is expressed by atheistic Communism's moral and social arson, and the clenched fist. The positive is expressed by Christianity's burning heart of love to God and mankind and the open hand of philanthropy and sacrificial service.

Let us never forget that the Early Church did not get going until it was set on fire with the Holy Spirit. A modern illustration is that of John Wesley. Wesley did not get going until he was Spirit-filled. When his heart became "strangely warmed," that made all the difference. He became "all burned up" about the evils and wrongs of his own day.

To counter our social and national enemies we need the enthusiasm for Christ and the gospel that Patrick Henry had for freedom and for America. When others were fearful, he declared: "Is life so sweet, and peace so dear, that it can be bought for the price of chains and slavery? God forbid! I know not what others may do, but as for me, give me liberty or give me death!" Such enthusiasm knows no defeat, transforms drudgery into pleasure, difficulties into possibilities, frustration into victory.

After the Pittsburgh Pirates had won the World Series, Dick Groat, the captain, was asked, "How did you do it against such tremendous opposition?" Groat replied, "It was because our team had unbeatable enthusiasm. Enthusiasm does something for every man on the team. It makes him daring, helps him overcome mistakes, and it conquers complacency." This is true in America's conflict with atheistic Communism. Just before Gary Cooper died, he was speaking about his success, with his accustomed modesty. "You've got to have a fire under you when you're a beginner," he said. "In fact, you've got to have a fire under you all the time."

That is excellent advice to young Christian ministers— yes, and to American businessmen and students as well.

Not long ago, I was invited to speak at Calvary Baptist Church in New York City. I arrived on a Saturday night. As is my custom, I took a walk around the area served by the church. It was a bitterly cold winter night. When I came to the corner of 57th Street and the Avenue of the Americas, a young woman, standing in that bleak nearly zero wind, handed me a tract. I refused it. When I arrived at a room, I could not help wondering just what that young woman was giving out. So I put on my coat again and went to see if she was still there. She was there. The wind had greatly increased. It was a terrible night. She offered me a tract again. I accepted it. When I got to my room again, I read it. To my dismay, I discovered it was not a gospel tract; it was one about Communism and why I should be a Communist.

Some weeks after that, I was invited to address a young people's conference. The president had assured me that there would be 2,500 young people present because it was their most important meeting of the year. After the president had introduced me, I said, "Mr. President, you told me you expected 2,500 young people here. I have hurriedly counted about 250." He replied, "Dr. Palmer, don't you know it is raining?" Of course I did. I had driven ninety miles in the worst kind of downpour. We sang "Like a Mighty Army"—and there were 2250 young leaders staying away because it rained!

I could not help thinking of that Communist girl standing in a blizzard propagating Communism. If the church fails in American life it will not be because of the enemies from without. It will be because of the absence of Christlike conviction and the burning heart within, expressing itself with a spiritual tongue of fire.

Our inner-space world can be conquered. It must be conquered. Do we really have what it takes? We must be optimistically minded, reckoning the future as glowing with victory for the kingdom of God.

Amid what Lowell called "the roar of advancing time," I challenge all to hold to our trust in God, to our faith, and to our conviction that Christ must reign, because I see that advancing future all aflame with the splendor of our resurrected, living and returning Christ. We can shake off all fear and look up to the hills of promise where the splendor and the glory of the triumph of the God in whom we trust shines upon their summits.

17

A Great American Need

> O that as our day is so may our strength be; that
> the men who are among us so highly endowed with
> integrity of character and honesty of conscience as
> well as with powerful talent and large experience
> may take their position upon the truth of God and
> abide by it at the last.
>
> *—Gladstone*

ONE CANNOT READ the story of Paul before Festus,
defending himself with warmth, positiveness and enthusiasm, without being convinced that here is a man who
knows what he is talking about (*Acts 24*). He evidently
has had a soul-upsetting experience which changed his
way of thinking and, therefore, his whole life.

Paul's defense was his experience. He told what had happened to him through his faith in Christ. He was not ar-
guing about the theories of salvation. He was telling Festus, the ruler, what he had experienced. Reasoning from
that experience he exhorted Felix, Agrippa, Drusilla and
others to give Christ a chance.

THE DEEPEST REALITY

Paul was using the method of the blind man whom Jesus healed. The blind man did not argue with his examiners. He said, "I do not know who it was that touched my eyes, or what kind of person he was, but this one thing I do know: whereas I was blind, now I see." We cannot get beyond a man's experience. How often have I said in my preaching: "It is easier to preach what we should practice than to practice what we preach." There is always a greater certitude in our message, a greater positiveness in our voice and a greater urgency in our appeal when we can say, "This I know because it has happened to me. I know what I was once, but since I let Christ come into my heart and life by simple trust, I have been a completely changed man."

The Bible is the book of enthusiasm. It creates enthusiasts when we accept its promises and make them part of our lives.

Listen to Isaiah, after he found the Lord. "I saw the Lord in the year King Uzziah died. He revealed himself to me and I cried, 'Woe is me, I am a man undone, a man of unclean spirit.' But God touched my lips, my tongue, my life, and I heard him say, 'Whom shall I send?' And I said, 'Here am I; send me!' " Then Isaiah gave us that great fifty-fifth chapter. "Come," he says, "you who thirst. Come take, eat that which is good. Eat and your soul shall live." He closes with these exultant words: "Ye shall go out with joy, and be led forth with peace. . . . The mountains shall break forth before you into singing, and all the trees of the field shall clap their hands."

David said, "I will bless the Lord at all times, his praise shall continually be in my mouth."

I am asking myself, "What is buoying us up in these depressing days? What spring breezes are refreshing us in this spiritual and moral humidity?" We need to get out of the grave clothes of depression, and put on the beautiful garments of joy, hope and praise. Depression is negation, weakness and defeat. Enthusiasm is positive, strong and victorious. Enthusiasm will remake us, if we give it a chance. Jesus was the great enthusiast. See how he speaks in difficulties: "Be of good cheer, I have overcome the world." He said that just before He went to the cross. "Because I have overcome," He said, "you, too, shall overcome. You can be victor with me. I will never fail you or forsake you." Christ is someone to be enthusiastic about.

GROW ROSES IN THE SOUL

My wonderful father was a great rose-grower. It was his hobby that kept him well and vigorous. The secret of his success as an amateur gardener was his enthusiasm. Everything he planted seemed to grow for prizes. His roses were the talk of the countryside. He exhibited his roses all over England and brought home prizes over the professional gardeners. His enthusiasm overcame all types of difficulties. He said to me one day, "Gordon, if you expect to grow roses, unusual roses, you must first grow roses in your soul." There you have it. We have to have a godlike gladness in our hearts if we would do what others cannot do.

There is my old friend, John Schreck, who was the superintendent of our Sunday school in Los Angeles. He retired from the telephone business years ago. He and his wife were wonderful Sunday school workers because they were enthusiastic about everything they did for the Lord. Many people after retirement grow dull, irritable, hard to get along with, lose all sense of mission; not John Schreck. John took up as a hobby the raising of singing canaries. And what marvelous success he has had! Mrs. Schreck was called home years ago. But John did not spend his time in grieving and complaining. He let his enthusiasm direct him. He has some of the most outstandingly beautiful canaries I have ever seen. His enthusiasm helped him over all kinds of difficulties. I visited him some time ago and he had his gramophone playing a record of canary songs so that his own little birds might imitate them—and they do. He has won scores of blue ribbons and gold cups for his prize birds. He is over eighty, but as young as fifty. He inspires everyone who visits him, because he has a great faith in God.

IN GOD IS OUR TRUST

When we study the epistles, we find the favorite expression Paul uses is "in Christ," or "Christ in you." When we are "in Christ," then we are "in God." When Christ is in us, God is in us. This enables us to be enthusiastic about our life, work, services, witnessing. It stirs us to be enthusiastic about everything we do for God and our fellow men. In this faith we can succeed, can be happy in an extraordinary manner. Our world has too many people who are carrying wet blankets of depression with them to put out the fire of enthusiasm.

For conquer we must
When our cause it is just,
And this be our motto
"In God is our trust."

We all need to tune up our faith in God until we know that in God we *do* trust. In Him we live and from Him get our vitality; in Him we move and get our power; and in Him we have our being and get our enthusiasm, which will help us do the impossible. This means that we have vigor, vitality and enthusiasm according to our trust in God.

Americans have power to overcome atheistic Communism and all other enemies in proportion to our trust in God. When we get out of harmony with God by our failing trust in him, then our enthusiasm fades away, our spiritual vitality declines and our political leadership with it. Many of us felt a serious lack of enthusiasm for the American free way of life and the old American freedoms in many of the speeches during recent election campaigns. That lack can never overcome the hates, the deceptions and the tyranny of our country's enemies. Our new leadership must get in harmony with righteous law and righteous principles, with God's unseen powers and with God Himself. Then we shall see the political, social, moral and spiritual leadership of America take on a new enthusiasm and a vitally transforming power.

18

Atheism—the Opiate
of the Communists

> . . . The god of this world hath blinded the minds
> of them which believe not, lest the light of the
> glorious gospel of Christ . . . should shine unto
> them.
>
> *—2 Corinthians 4:4*

ONE OF THE GREAT national magazines recently por-
trayed in beautiful colors the Red Square in Moscow. In
the center of the picture was Lenin's tomb, behind which
was a large building, advertising in the Russian language
this slogan: "Religion, the opiate of the people." That
Marxian declaration is a rallying call of the Communists in
their crusade to overthrow, if possible, all religion and especially the Christian religion.

Although the Communists demand that anti-God, anti-
church, anti-religion propaganda be crammed into the
minds of their children and youth as well as older people,
nevertheless, there seems to be evidence of a strong religious interest among large groups of Russians.

Adlai Stevenson, after a visit to Russia declared that "there were strong evidences of a vital religious life in Russia." Christians are challenged to undertake a great crusade of prayer that God shall strengthen these Russian Christians and send upon them such great spiritual grace and power that it will overtake the whole Russian people.

ATHEISM THE OPIATE

Instead of religion being "the opiate of the people" there is greater evidence that atheistic Communism is the opiate. Atheism is a mental drug, negative and sterile, lacking in inspiration and freedom. Atheism is the conscription of minds to negatives, a deadening of thought and an intellectual perversion.

According to medical authorities, "Opium is one of the most useful and one of the most harmful drugs. It readily creates a craving for itself. Opium produces sleep, but the onset of somnolence may be preceded by a certain amount of excitement. The victim of the opium habit loses his appetite and powers of digestion and, as a rule, his moral sense is progressively sapped until he becomes a liar and probably a thief; sometimes he loses his reason."

Apply this medical description of opium and its effects to atheistic Communism. Did not Jesus say that "Your eye is the lamp of the body. When your eye is sound, and fulfilling its office, your whole body is full of light: but when it is not sound and is not fulfilling its office, your body is full of darkness." (*Luke 11:34*)

We also remember that Paul the Apostle said, "The god of this world has blinded the unbelievers' minds (that they should not discern the truth) preventing them from seeing the illuminating light of the gospel of the glory of the Messiah, who is the image and likeness of God." (*2 Corinthians 4:4*)

That is the effect produced by atheistic Communism. Its victims lose the power to discern the truth. They become blind to it and fall into a moral sleep, disregarding the claims of human morality and personal dignity.

There are evidences of the loss of this moral sense during the voting of the Communist delegates at the United Nations. When other nations have been unanimous on scores of occasions, the Soviet delegates have vetoed the decisions more than eighty times. Although the majority of nations felt that their decisions would aid in the betterment of all and definitely promote the cause of world peace, Soviet delegates have employed their veto to stop them. Is not this evidence of the loss of their moral sense, to say nothing of their reason?

THE EVIL WORK OF SUPPRESSION

The Hungarian tragedy of 1956, when tanks and machine guns silenced the cries for liberty of the Hungarian people and murdered Hungarian nationals who were simply asking for the rights of life, liberty, and the pursuit of happiness, is clear evidences of the atheistic Communists' lack of reason.

Our President has declared that Communists have disregarded their so-called "sacred pledges" in over forty instances. All of these actions are evidence that they have imbibed the immoral opiate of atheism which has "blinded their eyes" to the needs of men and the peace of mankind.

The Communist code of immorality declares that the

end justifies the means. Therefore, they have resorted to "lies and deception without compunction" to gain their end. I quote from Lenin's writings (*Collected Works*, Vol. 17, pp. 142 ff.):

"A communist must be prepared to make every sacrifice and, if necessary, even resort to all sorts of schemes and stratagems, employ illegitimate methods, conceal the truth, in order to get into trade unions, stay there, and conduct their revolutionary work within. . . ."

We are seeing this declaration made effective today. The opiate of atheistic Communism has made the Communists lose their appetites for and their powers of digestion of the truth. The Bible puts it this way: "The god of this world has blinded their eyes so that they do not discern the truth."

Opium is said to blind the minds of men and make them insensitive to the sacredness of human life and personality. At the time of the Soviet's suppression of Hungary, the United States Congress unanimously adopted a resolution expressing America's "deep sense of indignation" over the murder of the Hungarian patriots.

David Lawrence has declared in an editorial: "The Communists are engaged in a desperate game of deception. They are actively trying to infiltrate and subvert the free governments of the world." These actions are evidence that the people who perpetrate them are under a demoniac power.

During the past few years the world has seen cities and

whole countries taken from the people by Communist deception, infiltration, and force. Their "dialectic" benumbs the conscience and makes them insensitive to truth, to honor, and to the sacredness of treaties. They seem to be controlled by the "prince of this world" whose business is to "blind the eyes of those who believe not."

Dr. Frederick Charles Schwartz, physician and psychiatrist, gave strong evidence before the House Committee on un-American Activities, May 29, 1957, that atheistic Communism causes loss of reason. I quote from the Committee's report:

> Mr. Weil asked Dr. Schwartz, "You think Khrushchev still believes in the classic theories as you expounded them?"
>
> Dr. Schwartz: "I believe that paranoia is at the heart of Communism and that their theoretical concepts are far more convincing to them than the evidence of facts. I believe, for example, that they, in their own minds, believe that the riots in Hungary were organized by the vicious American imperialists. There is this element of paranoic self-deception at the heart of Communism. I do not think they are hypocrites; they have merged the techniques of hypocrisy with the virtues of sincerity, creating a very powerful instrument. . . .
>
> "That insanity is manifest in the world hysteria they stirred up about the Rosenbergs. . . .
>
> "We have established that inherent within Communist ideology there is a program of murder, treachery, and brutality and that the theory of Communism

translates these acts into highly moral acts. The theory of Communism destroys every basic moral value on which civilization, and particularly Christian civilizaton is built." (*U.S. Government Printing Office, pp. 7, 8*)

When the Russian leaders declare they have thrown God out of their thinking, they actually admit that they are blind to the great virtues of truth, honor, justice, and liberty. They are "blind leaders of the blind."

A GLARING CONTRAST

How vastly different is the inspiration of the Christian religion, which the Communists call "the opiate of the people."

This faith is centered in Jesus Christ who declares that human life is sacred. Said He, "I am come that they might have life and that they might have it more abundantly." He urges His followers to dedicate their lives to the service of others. He makes it possible for broken men to be born again. He holds out hope and opportunity to those who have muddied-up their lives. He assures them that through true repentance and faith in Him they can become pure, provident, useful and strong. Christ taught that through the Christian Fatherhood of God there is the grand possibility of having a true brotherhood of man, where men will "bear one another's burden and so fulfill His law."

In this teaching are found social justice, personal integrity, humanitarian service, and freedom. Such is not found in Communism.

The Christian Gospel is diametrically opposite to the

dialectic of the atheism of Communists, which produces determined materialism. The Communist pushes God out of his thinking, therefore out of his life and consequently out of his morals.

Read the books *I Chose Freedom* and *Russia's Iron Age,* and you will see there is nothing in history comparable to the brutal methods used by the Communists in their crusade for world conquest and the enslavement of peoples. The Communist gives no value to the individual person. He thinks supremely in terms of the mass. The only thing that matters to him is the perpetuation of a group of men in imperialistic and despotic power "who are blinded by the god of this world."

Christianity has built its kingdom around the child. Our Lord put the child in the midst, saying "of such is the kingdom of heaven." The home—the Christian home—secures the healthy life of the people in the philosophy of Jesus. In contrast with this ideal, Communism thinks nothing of breaking up the family; controlling and directing the activities of fathers, mothers, sons, and daughters. When children are old enough they become the disciplined slaves of the Communist state.

The Christian religion believes in "the Godly-World-State" called "the Kingdom of God"; and every individual, no matter how good or how bad he may be, through penitence, faith, willing restitution, and Christian service, may enter into that Kingdom here and hereafter.

Thus, Christ establishes this Kingdom through the free choices of the people, giving them the privilege to accept or to reject Him and his Gospel.

When this freedom is exerted to its fullest under the beneficent power of Christ, according to the teaching of the Christian Gospel, men become truly free. This freedom guarantees a spiritual equality in the world, which is the foundation of our democracy.

This Christian freedom modifies for good all of our attitudes toward each other. It motivates our spiritual brotherhood. It builds harmony within the home, the community, the state, and in the world.

TO CONCLUDE

We have looked at both the dialectic of atheistic Communism and the Gospel of Jesus Christ. We find nothing of the opiate within the Christian faith.

The Christian religion does not benumb men's consciences nor send them to sleep in the presence of manifest moral and spiritual wrongs. The Gospel does not create a race of liars and thieves. Christians will lay down their lives for the truth, for "life, liberty, and the pursuit of happiness." When the Christian religion becomes a vital part of their lives, they do not lose their reason; they become more sensitive to the rights of others. In the Christian religion we see the hope of the world, and know that Christ is the answer.

Atheistic Communism stands as a challenge to Christians everywhere to take Christ and His Gospel seriously and to dedicate their lives in supreme commitment for God and country and humanity.

19

Our Fundamental
Belief in God

"In God We Trust" is foundational to a happy,
fruitful and dynamic American way of life at its
best.

AT THE BASE of the Freedoms Foundation "American Way of Life Credo" monument, is the giant foundation stone on which is engraved "Fundamental Belief in
God." All of the political and economic rights of man, as
well as those guaranteed by the Constitution of the United
States, are shown to be based in this "Fundamental Belief
in God."

Long ago, in the beginning of Hebrew history, a great
statesman declared, "If thou shalt harken diligently unto
the voice of Jehovah thy God to observe and to do all of
His commandments which I command thee this day, that
the Lord thy God shall set thee on high above all nations
of the earth" (*Deuteronomy 28:1*). The persistence of
the Jews in spite of the stupendous changes in the history

of nations is largely due to their belief in God. If America would hope to survive and continue her benevolent ministry to the world, she too must keep God in her thinking and her daily life.

WE DO NOT HAVE TO PROVE THAT GOD EXISTS

The Bible does not try to prove God's existence. The great assumption is that God does exist, that He is the rewarder of them who diligently seek after Him. The first word in the Bible is not "In the beginning we are going to prove that God exists." No! It begins with the majestic assumption, "In the beginning God." Without faith in God there would never have been an America. It is possible to show from history that God has had direct dealings with the founding of this country and with its magnificent history of world benevolence.

Let us not be confused and deluded by the reasonings and methods of the atheist who declares "There is no God." Actually, atheists do have a god. It is the god of Materialism, and that god has blinded their minds so that they do not, or will not, see that man is "made in the image of God." "God has put eternity into the heart of man," regardless of what they say about man being just another animal. Americans who inform themselves concerning the ideology of atheism and follow it to its logical conclusion will see it leads to suicide, personal and national. Karl Marx' daughter and his son-in-law committed suicide, exactly as they had planned years before. They were outspoken atheists. Biblical history declares, "The nations that forget (repudiate God) shall perish."

The God-controlled nation can and will win. It shall put its enemies of hate, violence, vice, and all evil under its feet.

THE PROVIDENTIAL IN OUR HISTORY

A few evidences of the movement of God in American history will help to substantiate the Freedoms Foundation declaration that our country's human rights are established on our "Fundamental Belief in God."

All devout historians believe that God had a hand in guiding Christopher Columbus, who was directing his ship straight for Delaware Bay, when a flock of birds was observed flying southwest. We are told that Pinzon persuaded Columbus to change his course and follow after the flight of birds. He did just that, and set his sails toward that new land which is now called San Salvador.

Cynics may say there is nothing to that story. However, Columbus did go south and took San Salvador in the name of King Ferdinand of Spain; which king, history declares, misruled the countries he controlled. That act of Columbus ultimately saved America from the blight of union with a foreign church and state. Thus, finally, the United States of America became the country where there was freedom to worship God according to the dictates of one's own conscience, and where a grand new free people was born. The Founding Fathers' belief in God inspired them to build, on this continent, "a new nation under God." Some fundamental things conform to the Bible pattern in our fundamental governmental life.

SOME FUNDAMENTALS

1. The thirteen states do not seem to have come into being by accident. There is divine purpose in the beginning of America through the thirteen colonies. When we read our Bibles we find that the Hebrews under Moses had thirteen states, or "tribes," as they were called. We usually think of twelve tribes, but there were thirteen, because the tribe of Joseph was divided into Ephraim and Manasseh. Therefore, the United States and Israel have a like establishment of states in the beginning.

2. According to *Exodus 18.17ff*, the governing laws or constitution of Israel was chosen by the people. At Philadelphia, the Constitution of the United States of America was formed but it was submitted to the people for ratification, just as was the constitution governing Israel. Up to that time these were the only two national constitutions ever submitted to the people for ratification.

3. Israel did not allow a foreign-born citizen to become their ruler. The Bible declares "No foreigner shall ever rule over you." Our Constitution provides that "No foreign-born man or woman may become President of the United States of America."

4. Holy Scripture was the text book of Israel for its laws and life. For years the Bible was the only text book governing the conduct of the Colonies and the United States of America, and even for years after the Declaration of Independence.

5. From the Bible it seemed that no king should ever rule over Israel. And no king did so rule until the establishment of the kingdom; which certainly did not have the

approval of Almighty God. God allowed it "because of the hardness of their hearts." Trouble, however, followed all through their kingdom history.

6. Israel's rulers were chosen not because of the so-called "right of birth," but because of character-worth. Just so it became the policy in the United States; the people made the choice. Up to the time of David the people of Israel chose their leadership.

7. The fifty-five men who met in Philadelphia to frame the United States Constitution were representatives of the thirteen colonies and were chosen because of their character, intelligence, and patriotic qualities. God had a strong hand in guiding that group of men in their formation of the basic law of our land. Their work has been proven to be of divine quality, and a statesman of England said that "The U. S. Constitution was the finest piece of work ever struck off the brain of man."

MAKING GOD'S COUNTRY

One's personal experience of the guidance of God convinces that God was guiding in the creation of the Constitution. For days the delegates had met and could not agree. The large states especially Virginia, Pennsylvania, and Massachusetts advocated a national plan. The smaller states took the federal side. The altercations at the convention shocked Benjamin Franklin. After ten days of squabbling, Franklin arose in the convention and said: "Mr. President, how has it happened, Sir, that while groping so long in the dark, divided in our opinions, and now ready to separate without accomplishing the great objects of our meeting, that we have not hitherto once thought of humbly applying to the Father of Lights to illuminate our understanding? In the beginning of the contest with Britain when we were sensible of danger, we had daily prayers in this room for divine protection. Our prayers, Sir, were heard, and they were graciously answered." Then after a few further remarks, Benjamin Franklin moved: "Henceforth, prayers imploring the assistance of Heaven and its blessings on our deliberations, be held in this assembly every morning before we proceed with business."

They recessed. After three days they met again. After prayer the delegates came to agreement and the Constitution was adopted—the finest declaration of modern government principles ever adopted by any nation.

If it had been some minister of the Gospel who had requested prayer, or had made such a passionate appeal for divine help, people would have said that it was only emotional special pleading. Benjamin Franklin, however, was a practical, hard-headed philosopher and statesman, as were the other fifty-four delegates at that convention.

Thus we can say in the spirit of the Bible: "In the beginning of the United States of America—'God.'" Our upstanding statesmen have believed in God and have many times called upon Him in the hour of perplexity. America can well follow the experience and example of our statesmen forebears and keep carved in the physical and spiritual and moral superstructure of our American way of life the "fundamental belief in God."

Another evidence of our fundamental belief in God is found when Abraham Lincoln was assassinated and the future of the Union looked very dark. Then James A. Garfield stood on the balcony of the City Hall in New York, and stilled an angry crowd by quoting from the Word of God: " 'Clouds and darkness are about His throne,' but fellow citizens, God reigns, and the government in Washington still lives."

When I was a student in the University of California, President Theodore Roosevelt came to the Greek Theater and gave a series of lectures on the Bible. He believed in the God of the Bible and endeavored to build his life and his governmental ministry around that morality of the Bible. Woodrow Wilson believed God, called on Him for guidance and wisdom during World War I. Franklin D. Roosevelt called on God in the dark days of the depression and during World War II. Calvin Coolidge believed in God and declared that America was a Christian nation. Herbert Hoover, the Quaker, believed in God and that He gave him practical guidance; Mr. Hoover, thus, became the world's statesman-benefactor. There are many such examples in our history.

We citizens of this great nation must keep, as fundamental, our faith and trust in God. It is a mark of the highest folly to kick out one's faith in God or to encourage anyone to divest himself of faith in God, just because some craven materialists seem to be getting more publicity than they deserve.

NEED FOR PATRIOTIC THINKING

There is no need for patriotic Christian Americans to grow discouraged. History seems to be on the side of dedicated minorities who have faith in God. A striking promise comes to mind which says "one (dedicated man of faith) can chase a thousand (unbelievers) and two can put ten thousand (unbelievers) to flight" (*Deuteronomy 32:30*). The patterns of the world for good can be changed by fully-committed American Christian patriots. The important thing is, do we reveal our faith and trust in God by conforming our lives and our society to God's standards? America need not fear being overthrown by atheistic Communism if its citizens and statesmen fully dedicate their brains, characters, moral and spiritual power to God. We shall then know that faith in God is the victory that overcomes all the forces of evil in the world.

Washington, Jefferson, Lincoln, McKinley, Bryan, Garfield, Roosevelt, were among the great men who believed in God. They were forward-looking men, wholly dedicated, who gave their best because they believed the best was ahead. Let us determine to keep God in the American way of life, in American industry, in American education, in American labor and management and in American politics and government. We shall then courageously follow in the steps of those forefathers who made basic in their lives and in ours a fundamental belief in God.

20

A Challenge to
the Prophets of Gloom

> To anticipate the future glory of America from present hopes and prospects is ravishing and transporting to the mind. In this light we behold our country, beyond the reach of all oppressors, under the great charter of independence, enjoying the purest liberty; beautiful and strong in its union; the envy of tyrants and devils, but the delight of God and all good men; a refuge to the oppressed; the joy of the earth . . . Hail, my happy country, saved of the Lord! Happy land, emerged from the deluges of the Old World, drowned in luxury and lewd excess! Hail, happy posterity, that shall reap the peaceful fruits of our sufferings, fatigues, and wars! With such prospects, such transporting views, it is difficult to keep the passions or the tongue within the bounds of Christian moderation.
>
> —*Phillips Payson, A.M., of Chelsea: Mass. Election Sermon, 1778.*

O F *Psalms 23*, a modern scholar has recorded a part of his translation as follows:

He guides me by true paths, as he himself is true; my road may run through a glen of gloom, but I fear no harm, for Thou art beside me; thy club and thy staff, they give me courage.

There is no doubt that in history and in our own experience there are glens of gloom through which we must travel. However, it is a practice of many people to see nothing *but* "the glen of gloom." And that is opposite to the positiveness of the Gospel of God. He does not expect us to be oblivious of the darkness. He wants us to remember that darkness is always the absence of light. But He sent Jesus Christ to be the light of the world, the light of our nation, the light of our personal lives. And a direct statement of Jesus concerning His mission was, "I am come a light in the world that whoever believes in me may not walk in darkness." And again He said, "I am the light of the world: he who follows me shall not walk in darkness but will have the light of life."

It seems human to walk in the gloom—in the darkness. But God desires us to dwell in the light, to walk in the light, to live in the light, to give light. He does not desire us to be like the proverbial ostrich, to put our heads in the sand and stay there, as if there were nothing wrong with the world. There certainly have been dark days upon the face of the earth.

We in this country have traveled through many glens of gloom, some of them not too far remote from those described by H. G. Wells in his book, *Shape of Things to Come*. That book painted a dark picture indeed, but its author at least seemed to let man survive.

THIS NO PLACE FOR DESPAIR

I do not intend to try further to prove that there are dark sides to our world picture. Nor am I being a foolish Pollyanna when I say Christians can always challenge the prophets of gloom. Jesus said dark days would come, but He did not say, "Therefore, despair." On the contrary, He said, "When you see these things come to pass, look up, for your redemption draweth nigh." That does not look as if God intended Christians to travel all their lives through the "glen of gloom." However, if we insist on staying in the glen of gloom, God asks us to sing the shepherd's psalm, and joyfully express our faith in the Lord God omnipotent, who must reign. "Yea, though I walk through the valley of the shadow of death I will fear no evil, for Thou art with me. Thy rod and thy staff, they comfort me."

The Christian believer has nothing to fear, except fear. And we can overcome fear by a living, vital, glowing faith. Use the faith you have. It may not be much, but *use what faith you have;* then you will find God comes and increases that faith. You must keep and use your faith and your faith will keep you. If you do not use your faith—even the little faith you have—you will lose it. So declare, day by day, no matter how dark the glen, or the valley, or your life, "I will fear no evil, for Thou art with me." God is nearer to you than you believe. So, quit your unbelief, and claim God's blessed presence. Christ assures us that God is with us, for He says, "Lo, I am with you always."

Instead of practicing the cult of fear, practice the fact of faith. I must keep emphasizing this fact and the grand truth: This is the victory that overcomes the world of darkness, the world of your personal gloom; yes, the whole world of evil. "This is the victory that overcomes the world, even our faith."

THE BUOYANCY OF FAITH

When we live the life of faith we find that faith is the grandest and most effective therapeutic for healing known. Doctors cannot help us when they know they are faced with people of no faith in them or in their therapy. Faith puts spring into the step. Faith permeates every nerve and blood vessel and muscle and bone of the body and every phase of the mind and brain. The man of faith is the man of victory because he is the man at peace. Faith makes you look up when the gloom presses on you. Faith in God is the greatest antidote to every kind of fear. Faith is the victory that overcomes the world of all evil.

There is no doubt that the United States of America has come to its present position of material and spiritual power because America was founded by men of faith. Their Christian faith permeated their governmental theories, their moral demands, their educational institutions. Faith was the vital, the supreme, the secret weapon of our forefathers all through their struggles to establish a "new nation under God."

The Declaration of Independence was inspired by faith in God, in the laws of nature and nature's God. The Preamble to the Constitution is the expression of that faith in God and the laws of God to "form a more perfect union, to establish justice, to insure domestic tranquillity, to provide for the common defense, to promote the general welfare, and to secure the blessings of liberty to ourselves and our posterity. . . ." The Preamble is saturated with faith in God, because these blessings, privileges and principles cannot be attained or achieved without this living, vital, dynamic faith in God and our fellow men.

HISTORY'S MEN OF FAITH

Our whole history has been an expression of the faith of the men of God who, as citizens of the United States, have dedicated their lives to the achievement of these God-given and God-assured blessings. God has never failed any man or woman or people faithful to Him and obedient to His laws. Our forebears did not subscribe to Browning's easy dictum, "God's in His heaven, All's right with the world." Neither did they say, "Don't worry. Just relax. Just leave everything to God and it will come out all right." By no means. They did say, "Have faith in God, but also dedicate your lives to carrying out His will." And our history shows, as does biblical history, that whenever a nation, a people, or an individual, is obedient to the will and laws of God, God never fails them. They can say, "Though I walk through the valley of the shadow of death (or through the glen of gloom) I will fear no evil for Thou art with me."

We can never challenge the prophets of gloom by sentimental platitudes or by wishful thinking. It needs a faith in God backed by personal consecration to Him, full obedience to His laws, and submission to His guidance; then we can claim the promises of the living God to aid us and lead us to achieve "life, liberty, and the pursuit of happiness."

I like the faith, good cheer, and Christian optimism expressed by ex-President Herbert Hoover, who said: "There are voices in our country who daily sound the alarm that our civilization is on the way out. But civilization does not decline and fall while people still possess their dynamic, creative faculties, their devotion to religious faith and to liberty. The American people still possess these qualities. We are not at the bedside of a nation in death agony."

While there are tens of thousands of men and women like you men and women of faith who read these words, or listen to them on radio's Christian Patriotism broadcasts, and who, out of your small or large incomes, support causes like the Indian orphans, youth centers, churches, medical centers of research, and the like, it is only because you back your gifts with prayer and personal lives of faith that we have a spiritual survival power to overcome the forces of atheistic Communism and all forms of moral, physical, and spiritual delinquency.

Of course we must not, and cannot, shut our eyes to the clouds. They do often obscure the sun. But men of faith and Christian dedication have at their disposal something that atheistic Communism does not possess. We have faith in the living, personal, omnipotent, victorious God. When we do what Jesus said—"Look up"—we can see multitudes of things at work in our world that show these forces of faith are changing things for God and for good.

The church, with all of its weaknesses, is doing the best work it has ever done in reaching people for God and influencing men, women, and youth for righteousness. Humanitarian agencies are working feverishly to help solve the problems of delinquency, and the churches are co-operating to saturate these agencies with a dynamic, living faith. Industry and labor, with all of the un-Christian forces within them that make righteousness difficult, nevertheless have more of the Spirit of Christ working within them than ever before. We see too often only the Communistic influences at work. Christian men and women must double their energies within and without these great agencies to help the Christian principles dominate their relationships. We can see today, as God said to Elijah in his despondency, "There are still 7000 who have not bowed their knees" to the Baal of defeat and eternal gloom.

THE ETERNAL ASPECT OF FAITH

When we read anew the story of the resurrection of Jesus Christ, we see again His challenge to the prophets of gloom. His resurrection is the guarantee of spiritual and moral triumph of righteousness and dynamic faith, no matter where that faith may be expressed. No darker day in spiritual history was ever recorded than the day when the enemies of Christ nailed Him to the cross on Calvary. His disciples thought that was the end. The sun veiled its face during that tragic hour and darkness was all over the world. The disciples were so discouraged that they said, "We had hoped that it was He who should redeem Israel." It was the world's darkest, gloomiest hour. But when everybody thought all was lost, Jesus Christ came forth victor over death and hell. He revealed himself as the living Lord and Redeemer to his disciples. That revelation changed them. After the Holy Spirit came upon the disciples at Pentecost, the deadly persecution of Christ's followers did not discourage them. They were scattered abroad. But wherever they went they proclaimed the gospel of resurrection.

The Christian faith in eternal life is the supreme weapon against atheistic Communism and against every evil force in the world. We can and we must challenge the prophets of gloom by dynamic faith and consecrated Christian lives.

If your candle of faith is burning low, let Jesus Christ, the Light of the World, light up your candle. When William Sidney Porter, the American writer best known as "O. Henry," was dying, he said to his nurse, "Nurse, bring me a candle." "Why do you want a candle?" asked the nurse. O. Henry replied, "Because I am afraid to go home in the dark."

No man or woman, and no nation, need go home in the dark. If every Christian American will let the candle of his faith shine, backed by his fully dedicated life, God will furnish the wisdom, the spiritual power and understanding to make his "kingdom come and his will be done, on earth as it is in heaven." The light of our faith will win. God is with us!